Shadows
of
the
Summer
Solstice

Shadows of the Summer Solstice

--a Legend about a Farmer and the Green Ribbon Murder

By

Sharon Schaadt Cowen

DISCLAIMER

This story is being told as a legend. The bones of it are based on J. H. Day's booklet *Lynched*, blended with my father's version, and supplemented by my imagination. Most last names have been omitted because I wish no harm to any survivors. With the plethora of conflicting information from nearly a century and a half ago, I realize I may have unintentionally included erroneous components. For that I apologize. The events affected everyone involved for generations. Hopefully something good can still come from it.

Lily Illustration by Janice D. Cowen

Cover Photo by Sharon Cowen

SSC Publishing

ISBN13: 978-0-578-46094-9

ACKNOWLEDGMENTS

For my children and their spouses, Lyn and Jay, and Sara and Gary, and my grandchildren, Jarrett, Justine, Jhett, Ava and Connor.

This book is dedicated to the task, insurmountable though it may seem, of helping to tame humanity.

It is also dedicated to every child and adult who has encountered a predator, in particular, Mary, as well as Liberty German and Abigail Williams from Delphi, Indiana.

Thank you, Dad, for telling the story. Thank you, Judy and Karen, William Sitterley, and Karen's Chatt for your important input. An immense 'thank you' goes to Janice D. Cowen and Darci Leigh, (authors in their own right), as well as Sue Davidson, Shirley Ziemer, and Rebecca Golden for helping me see it through and see through it. Thank you to every relative, ancestor, friend, and connection who did the same. Thank you, Dr. Dennis E. Hensley and Tamara Szarszewski for the early edits. Thank you, J.H. Day and David Kimmel, for your work, and thank you to the amazing residents of Mercer County who survived this horror and remember it still.

I am deeply grateful to my Great Grandpa Fred for his examples of faith, hope, and love which saturate the centuries.

I wish no harm, but only good to come from this tragedy.

Table of Contents

Gardens don't care about catastrophe. Like in early Eden, no recognition of good or evil exists. Instead, plants convert sun, rain, air, and dust into life-sustaining food. Green never ceases or surrenders its mission. Even when humans spade in fields of hate and are stuck in emotional muck, gardens grow.

CHAPTER 1 – THE WAY IT WAS IN 1872

"As the terebinth tree and the oak leave stumps when they are cut down, so the holy seed will be the stump in the land."
Isaiah 6:13

Phil Kromer spoke in a gravelly voice. "Gonna tell yuh how it was, Tom. It was a big story, but it happened in a small place. I thought about startin' when Fred made the oak casket, but that's not really when it begun. It begun with harvestin' wheat."

Tom barely listened as he set about cleaning the old man's room. Tom's bosses didn't like the largest dwelling in the county dubbed "The Poor House." They preferred "The Adams County Infirmary" or, better yet, "Golden Meadows Home." In their effort to renew its image, the matron had directed the young custodian to wash every wall, ceiling, window, and floor so the place "sparkled and smelled like spring."

Water sloshed as Tom mounted a tall ladder. The young man positioned his galvanized bucket and wondered what kind of tale this rusty resident might spout. As far as he knew, Phil had never married, and a nephew, who visited infrequently, was his only living relative. He was sure the elderly man had never left the Midwest. The way the old coot maneuvered, he could scarcely muster the energy to leave his room.

Old Phil removed his gold-rimmed spectacles. The scratched lenses blurred his view of the present, but when he downed the bent frames, his past popped out of the bubbles Tom applied to the ceiling, and the previous century enlivened his stark surroundings.

His white chin stubbles reflected the morning sun. Phil rasped, "Let me tell yuh, Tom, 1872 spawned one hot summer. Sweat was the scent everyone was wearin'. The fields of wheat puffed-out, pregnant, and nearin' their time. If yuh wasn't workin' the farm, or washin' clothes, or makin' a pie fer supper, yuh was useless, or up to no good.

"This story starts and stops on Tama Road. My folks lived nearby. I was in my twenties. I'm in my eighties now, yuh know. Some of what I'm tellin' come firsthand, but the rest I reaped from others involved.

2

"Tama's spelled 't-a-m-a,' but it's pronounced 'Tame-uh,' like yuh'd tame an animal. From what I saw back then, we'd best work at peace-a-fyin' people from darkness.

"In only two weeks' time, the drama was mostly over, or so we thought. I bet I'll be finished with the tellin' 'fore you're finished washin' down them walls. I'll start with Saturday, June 22nd, 1872.

"A few clouds wrinkled the sky. Chickens huddled in their nests with their heads tucked 'tween their wings, and their eyes closed tight as Fred hoisted his grindstone onto his forearms and carried it from his barn into a crevice of mornin' light. He placed it on four familiar dents in the ground. It looked like an upside-down bicycle with the back wheel missin' and the front, a massive stone mounted higher than the seat.

"Like mosta the men in the Midwest, Fred farmed. He was big-muscled, but hard-work skinny. His body swayed at a steady pace as he sharpened the long metal blade of his scythe. It attached to an even longer wooden handle. Both of 'em curved like Fred's smile. The stone filed the metal, spittin' tiny sparks. It continued to spin even after Fred stopped pedalin'.

Fred's neighbor, John Sitterley, headed in his direction. Nothin' stood out about how Sitterley looked, a handsome man with light brown hair and kind eyes, 'cept once yuh met him, yuh'd not forget him. A little older than Fred, and also farmer

3

thin, John carted one fat sense of humor. Fred told me 'bout their conversation."

'You're at work extra early, Fred. Did you startle any chickens?'

'I got startled before the first rooster crowed. Yesterday I checked the wheat. I think come Monday I'll chop. Crop's ahead of schedule this year.'

'Since we planted on the same day, we should be close on time.'

"Fred edged the blade along the stone. A steady stream of water dripped from the point of a metal cone hangin' above the wheel.

"You can't sharpen good without water, huh, Tom? Seems like all shinin' up does best with it."

Phil took a drink from the glass on his bedside table allowing the liquid to swirl and cleanse and re-cleanse his tongue. The question had been Phil's test to see if his custodian was listening. His hesitation allowed him time to find out. He watched Tom nod in the affirmative even though the janitor's head tilted back to work the ceiling. Satisfied with the young man's efforts, the old man swallowed hard.

"Let's talk about Fred. His hair had a mind of its own. It flipped up on the ends, same as the cut of his smile with locks spoonin' up from behind each ear as if he was wearin' the roof of one of them oriental buildin's designed to whisk away the demons. On humid days, when he couldn't control it, he liked to say, 'I can't look any different than I look.' And on rainy days when it curled like a sprung spring, he'd claim, 'I'm not as dumb as I look.' He kept his beard short and well-trimmed as if to compensate...if not, who knows what direction it mighta took. His face was two different colors cause his wide-brimmed hat kept the sun off his forehead, but not his cheeks which was sunburnt and tanned so deep, the skin never did fade completely. Most farmers had the same kinda skin tones and looked both bleached and broasted.

"John Sitterley decided to stick around fer small talk until Fred finished sharpenin'. Though this isn't part of what happened, I'll be tellin' it, 'cause we've got time. It'll let yuh know a little about what Fred had at stake. John had somethin' to lose, too.

"Sitterley said, 'I remember watching you sharpen a broad ax with a giant blade and short handle your first winter here. Remind me again when and how it was you came to this neck of the woods.'

'Twenty-seven years ago. I'll do the math, John...the year was 1845. Our trip from Germany took about two months. We left because of the conscription. My father had served three years in the army. He decided none of his sons would be

5

bought for war. My grandfather watched Napoleon take our men as the French passed through Löllbach on their way to Waterloo.'

"John said, 'War is awful. I hope you never have to kill anyone, Fred.' Then his eyes got a far-away look. John had served in the Civil War. Any loud bang made him skittish. Them memories drove him to work nearly non-stop to keep his mind off the horrors he'd seen. He could never speak of 'em directly.

'I was born here, Fred. I don't recollect a trip or a ship. Tell me more.'

'I was four when we left and five when we landed. The pine trunk we have in our cabin contained everything my family owned. My dad, along with my namesake, Uncle Frederick, made it special for the voyage. Sometime I'll show you the dovetailing. I was glad not to get lost at sea because the Atlantic looks the same in all directions when the sky's clouded. Often her waves arched higher than a bucking horse. I remember how the ups and downs pushed us across the planks, especially my sisters and me since we were small. I worried, *What if those glassy waves break and our ship goes right through to the bottom?* Not a one of us could swim.

It took awhile to get our sea legs, and then to get rid of them again when we came ashore to file for citizenship. Headed down the gangplank, we weaved side to side, and I accidentally stepped on my mother's dress causing both of us to tumble. The minute we touched the ground, I waved good-bye forever to the blue sea and said a happy hello to a sea of green.'

"Fred developed a rhythm to his process. His words blended with the whir of the grindstone.

'You spent a long time on the ship. I can't imagine you going without good food for two days, let alone two months, Fred. What did you have to eat?'

"Fred wrinkled his nose. 'The ship's kitchen served a lot of sauerkraut. The crevices in the floorboards swallowed it when stomachs didn't settle. I can still remember the smell.'

'How'd it happen you inherited the trunk?'

'It was the same length I was. My dad joked in broken English, "When we get to new country, this be right size for bed for Fred.'

'I figure you still might have to sleep in it when you and Kate have a tiff,' John chuckled. I'm trying to recall how long you said you worked to buy your first land.'

'I carpentered for four years until I could afford wooded ground at Convoy. All I ever wanted to do was farm. My new land didn't have a spot big enough to plant a seed, let alone a plow. Tree by tree I cut through thicker lumber than any I'd carpentered. I didn't keep count of the falling timbers or flying

7

wood chips I dodged. My younger brother helped me use the crosscut saw. Once I hung my coat on a limb while he and I burned a brush pile. He chattered non-stop. What a schnodderbox. I told him not to talk so much, because we had work to do. I said, "Think three times before you speak again." When he noticed smoldering, he said, "I think. I think. I think your coat's on fire!"

'With five acres finally ready to farm, I sold at a profit, bought a new coat, and laid out the first payment for the land of my dreams right here on Tama Road.'

'You got quite a bargain, Fred…twelve acres, already cleared, and me as your neighbor. These weren't the only deals you were after though, now were they?'

'No, I was bargaining for Kate. But I had another problem.'

'You had a place to live on, but no place to live in?'

'It's the language of the birds…first you build the nest, then you begin the life. I bought in October and right away began work on our cabin. Meanwhile, Kate's parents let me stay with them. Kate's dad kept telling me "Don't put the cart before the horse." He wouldn't have let me marry her come winter if I didn't have a nest ready.'

'I recollect seeing her pa help you fell trees. Who was he trying to get rid of, you or Kate'?"

'Probably the both of us.'

'Yes, I remember how you sat at this grindstone…only instead of a scythe you sharpened the broad ax I spoke of earlier. The blade was nearly as long as the handle. You used it to remove the bark.'

'I had to. Kate wouldn't have tolerated it crumbling onto the cabin floor. The ax's blade started out a lucky thirteen inches long and eight inches wide. Now it's only seven and seven-eighth's inches wide. I peppered the snow with a lot of iron.'

'Considerin' the size of the ax, it's a wonder you have any fingers left. I figure you left some knuckle shavings, too.'

"Fred eyed his hands and said, 'Not much gone. The handle is curved to give finger room and follow the bend of the trees. I'll bet your dad did the same.'

John teased, 'And I thought the handle bent because you couldn't cut straight. I've always supposed the new cabin warmed you three times, Fred. First, from using the hefty ax, and again when you started a fire in the hearth, and last, but I betcha not least, when you moved in with your beautiful bride.'

'I figure you remember helping raise our cabin out of the February snow, John…best time for a change in temperature. I married Kate on her birthday at the end of the month. Best time to hibernate.'

'You're blushing, Fred.'

"Fred returned his freshly sharpened scythe to the barn. He lugged in the heavy grindstone. 'A place fer everything and everything in its place,' he said.

'All joshing aside, what do you say we check our wheat? But before we do, if you've got a minute, come in and see the dovetailing.'

"Inside their cabin, four-year-old Phebe and three-year-old Anton played on the floor. Baby Emma slept in the walnut cradle. Kate offered cookies. The smell of fresh-baked bread invited more tastin'. Fred loved Kate's cookin'. Nothin' burnt ever come from her kitchen.

'Thanks, Kate. You and Sarah both bake fine goods. Not a better smelling neighborhood can be found anywhere. Someday Fred and I will be so fat, we'll have to roll over to check our wheat.'

"Fred noticed John Sitterley wistfully glance at their children.

"John said, 'This is fine dovetailin,' Fred.'

"Kate's face flushed, only adding to the beauty of her flawless skin and blue eyes. Their talk and John's attention to the little ones made Fred think about his three most treasured possessions. Other'n his family, who he didn't call a possession, and his land, the trunk, the broad ax, and the cradle come in first. Fred loved to say, 'My past is in a pine trunk, my present is in an oak cabin, and my future is in a walnut cradle. I saved my finest wood for my future.'

"Yep, Fred was particular, and he was proud, maybe too proud, 'cause pride kin come right before a fall, yuh know. Though, with him, maybe it weren't gist pride. In his later years, I heard Fred say, 'I'm living my life like a ten-cent millionaire.'

"The two men headed over to John's field hopin' when they bit down on a grain, they'd hear gist the right crack indicatin' their crops was near ready. Each broke off a stem. Startin' at the top, they stripped the grains. Cuppin' the gold clusters in their palms, they blew out the chaff. Both men put a seed between their teeth and crunched."

"John said, 'Looks like come Monday we'll start chopping.'
'Better sharpen your scythe, John."

"At the moment Fred begun his sentence, a large wagon rattled into sight. Fred fixed his words to fit the happenin'.

'Guess I'm not the only one doing some pedaling today. Better sharpen your scythe and loosen yer wallet, John. Here comes the tin peddler.'

"As the huckster approached, a murder of crows cawed their way to a nearby tree."

CHAPTER 2 — GRANDPA STROUSE'S FAMILY

As deep as the wound is, is as deep as the healing can go.

Phil rested his wire-rimmed spectacles on his bedside table. Tom noticed him slowly spin the gold frames. As they rotated, Phil seemed to be stirring his connection with the past. Tom figured the twirling brought up heavy pieces long-settled in the old man's story pot. The young janitor had begun to find some interest, and occasionally paused to listen, letting water drip, drip, drip into the bucket before he wrang out the rag.

"I'm gonna talk now about how it was a little further to the east down Tama road. Grandpa Strouse and his wife lived on the north side. Their daughter, Susannah, had married Joseph. He come from France. Susannah birthed four children I know of…Calvin, Elias, and then a set of brown-eyed twins, a boy and a girl, named Marion and Mary. Everyone knew 'em, 'cause to have survivin' twins was a big deal back then. They was the only twins on Tama Road. People liked to say their names together 'cause of the ring. 'Mar-y and Mar-ion, Marion and Mary.'

"But Susannah never did recoup from the double-birthin'. Joseph wasn't able to deal with a sickly wife, two hollow-legged boys, and them two new babies. Grandpa and Grandma Strouse did their best to help, takin' all six into their house to live.

"When the twins turned ten, Susannah died. Joseph up 'nd left, but to make his journey easier, didn't take no children. Calvin and Elias was thought old enough to fend fer themselves. It was the twins what needed new homes 'cause Grandma was ailin'and walked too feeble to care fer two ten-year-olds with growth spurts comin' on. As I remember, Marion went to relatives who gist wanted the boy.

"Who would take Mary? Most people preferred fellas instead of females to help on the farm. It was Grandpa Strouse who thought to ask the Sitterleys, since John and Sarah didn't have no children. Sarah was so tiny. It wasn't any wonder she was barren.'

CHAPTER 3 — MARY

It was time for the lilies to bloom. Some don't flower as long as others. A particular one, the fragile daylily, lasts briefly as its name implies. To compensate for their imminent demise, swarms of them cluster in the ditches. Rapidly taking turns, they add an orange luster to roads otherwise coated in dust and mud and bordered in shades of green.

Tom hadn't noticed how much soot from the infirmary furnace had catapulted straight to the ceiling. Since he began right above a register, the water in his cleaning bucket quickly became murky and needed dumping. He figured he'd refresh it before Phil got any farther into telling his tale, though the janitor could see the old man preferred not to be delayed. A growing sense of urgency crept into Phil's voice and posture. Tom's ladder screeched as he repositioned it.

Phillip resumed in a more solaced tone. "Let's talk about the girl. This part comes from some of her friends and a little from what Sarah Sitterley 'ventually could speak of herself.

She loved orange lilies…prob-ly 'cause her life had been fallin' gist like their petals. Somehow they gave Mary comfort, tellin' her she weren't alone in the losses after all.

"It was when Susannah died the first petal dropped, leavin' the biggest hole in the blossom. Mary and her mamma was real close, her bein' the only girl and all.

"Within a week or so, Joseph departed, and Marion got took by the relatives—two more gone. With Calvin and Elias on their own, Mary 'Belle, sometimes they called her 'Belle,' was the last and only of her immediate family remainin' on Tama Road. It all happened so fast, gist like the life of them lilies.

"As an orphan and a sweet girl by nature, she became the darlin' of the neighborhood. She had brown hair, and a few freckles. People would comment about Belle's eyes.

"Since they lived close, she already knew John and Sarah. Though she adjusted, and the Sitterleys give her this lovely home, people said the girl always seemed a little sad.

"Mary's friends told how she liked to play with words. She would say, 'I have a 'May' in my family, but not a 'June,' She would wonder, 'How did the Sitterleys git their name since they rarely sit?' She come up with the idea, 'Maybe someone in their past joked about them, like the way the kids at school call heavy-set James, 'slim Jim.' She even noticed the word 'tame' in Testament and marveled about it and livin' on

'Tame-uh' Road, and she broke it down like this: *'Test-tame men-t'*. She was a thinker, that girl.

"At thirteen, Belle 'spected the next year would be her last year educatin'. The eighth grade usually was fer rural children back then. When graduation came the followin' spring, it'd be time to enter the world of work fer both boys and girls. Marion would farm. Mary wouldn't see him much. She might clean houses or care for new babies. She didn't know John and Sarah had thought to git her more schoolin' so as, if she wanted or needed, she could be a teacher. Life as she'd knowed it was definitely droppin' away.

"Sarah Sitterley quickly become the bright spot in Mary's day. Sarah's nurturin' instincts was strong. It matched Mary's memory of her mama. Sarah bought the girl two lovely Sunday-go-to-meetin' dresses. Most country girls her age owned only one, and it was often homemade.

"Mary also owned beautiful jewelry, includin' a set of pearls and a fine locket. The gold locket was hand-engraved with what I heard called a 'fleur de lis' curvin' round the top and down the bottom again. 'Fleur de lis' is French words, yuh know? 'Mighta been to honor her pa."

Tom nodded.

"Next to the fleur and some cross-hatchin' was a crescent moon inset with a row of tightly packed sparklin' stones.

16

Looked like diamonds, they did. A tiny bird with a red garnet or perhaps even a ruby eye took up the center. The little creature was in flight. I saw the piece myself. It stayed in Mary's family with the survivin' brothers. I think it went to the oldest.

"Some say Mary kept a lock of her mama's hair inside. She opened it often to gaze. I'm guessin' she got the jewelry special fer keepin' the blond-brown hair when her mama died, or maybe it was Mary's own hair from the first time she had it trimmed. It coulda even been her mama's locket to begin with. I don't know any of this fer a fact…gist know she had the locket 'cause I seen it myself. It was unusual fer a young girl on Tama Road to have such a lovely piece.

"Only a week or so before the incident, Sarah Sitterley and Mary had stopped by Maggie's store to look fer a hat to match her Sunday dresses. Maggie had gist the one. Sarah said, 'I want you to add strong ties so if any wind comes along, Mary's bonnet won't fly off into the dust or mud and get ruined.'

"They picked a No. 9 green, grosgrain ribbon, one and a half inches wide. It made a beautiful thick bow. Mary's friends said the fabric smelled like lavender. To boot, Mary had a parasol. Sarah saw to it no sun or rain would ever bother her.

"Yuh know, Tom, I've wondered through the years if Mrs. Sitterley thought all the new things would help Belle replace them lost petals."

CHAPTER 4—SATURDAY EVENING

By Saturday evening, a moon glowed with an open yellow throat ready to swallow the speckled night sky.

"A full moon popped out on Friday, but still looked round on Saturday."

As Phil spoke, a soapy glob dropped from the ceiling and plopped onto the old man's spectacles. Tom apologized and climbed down to clean them. While Tom dried the lenses, Phil continued...

"Saturday was bath night on the farm. Bucket by bucket, Belle pumped water to fill the tub. Everyone in the house used the same water—too much siphonin' and carryin' and heatin' to have it any different. Things got conserved 'cause of the amount of energy it took to git 'em. Since you have to carry water, too, Tom, I bet yuh understand."

A nod was all Tom could interject before Phil began his next sentence.

"John and Sarah owned a big copper tub. It set in a separate room. An order existed for bathin'. The cleanest went first and the dirtiest last. Some did their soakin' in the opposite direction, but cleanest to dirtiest kept the water freshest—Mary first, then Sarah, then John. No one ever commented about how the first toe-wetter had worked the least, and it was the reason they was cleanest. It woulda been a backhanded remark to say anythin' of the sort. Work done was how people was judged, yuh know.

"It wasn't Mary was so spoiled she did nothin'. She did her chicken chores…feedin' and waterin', and gatherin' and washin' the eggs.

"Phebe saw her outside and called, 'Mary, Mary, can you come over and play?' Mary answered, 'I have to do work today. Tomorrow's Sunday. I'll come after church and you've had your naps. I promise.'

"Mid-morning, Belle helped Sarah with the baking and the dishes. Sarah told how rollin' out pie crusts, and cuttin' pretty vent patterns fer the steam, and crimpin' the doughy edges gave Mary pride. They made the crusts of fresh lard and flour, and a little water and salt, but Sarah also added a dash of vinegar.

"Mary liked the crust better without the vinegar, not because of the taste, but 'cause of the smell, and 'cause a brown glob called 'mother of vinegar' floated in the bottom of the jug. It looked nasty. Mary's friends said she couldn't bear the thought of accidentally touchin' it.

"Mary asked, 'Why do they call it 'mother?' One of the girls told her, 'It's because it looks like afterbirth.' Mary cringed. 'I know Mama wasn't well after she birthed Marion and me.'

"Sarah reminisced how Mary also enjoyed bakin' bread. She loved kneadin' the loaves and watchin' 'em grow flesh-colored in the pans. She liked to pat the fat belly. Some of the batter would become sweet rolls fer a quick Sunday breakfast to give extra time to git ready fer church. No one ate a sit-down breakfast on Sunday.

"Mary told Sarah, 'The smell of bread bakin' makes up for the vinegar in the pie crust.' Seems the girl always tried to soothe over somethin' she didn't like.

"Mrs. Sitterley remarked how the sunset on Saturday was streaked with all of Mary Belle's favorite colors. Belle favored watchin' the sun over milkin' the cows. She dreaded gettin' swatted by their bony tails, 'specially when the long hairs on the ends had been dipped in fresh manure and painted her pretty face.

"Mary Belle also loved the stars. She pretended one of the salt specks in the Big Dipper was where her mama was now.

"As I was sayin', the weekend when the misfortune happened, the moon was full. People say not only does it pull the tide, but it kin yank a post right out of the ground. We had a neighbor once who built his fence in its light hopin' his posts would draw up like the ocean, and all our baby pigs would slip under to his side. My dad and me had to reset the whole fence.

"The moon has scary powers, yuh know, 'specially on them who's up to no good.

"On Saturday evening, when Mary climbed onto her feather tick, it was extra soft. Sarah had plucked down from their geese to fluff her pillow.

"The girl was tired enough to sleep, but alert enough to remember her dream when she awakened. The images scared her. Even in the swelterin' heat of late June, she woke shivering so hard she thought she might shake all the freckles off her cute little nose. Havin' been told 'not to tell her dreams before breakfast lest they might come true,' she ate her sweet roll first."

CHAPTER 5 – THE RAILROAD ELECTION

Disorder has claws and a snarl.

Old Phil closed his eyes, seeming to take a nap, and maybe start a dream of his own. Tom continued working quietly so as not to disturb him. The silence lasted only a few minutes when the sudden volume, fervor, and sounds of impending danger in Phil's voice nearly shook Tom off the ladder.

"No soft lullabies followed the railroad election. The smells of iron, tobacco, and liquor blended in a weighty brew. Fierce shoutin' could be heard over the clankin', poof, bell, and smell of any incomin' engine. People heard a voice say, 'You think you know it all! I've seen and done way more than any of you ever will!'

Alexander Mcleod hollered at his co-peddler, Andrew Jaxton, also jokingly known as 'The President,' and at Andy's two cousins, short Absalom and tall Jake.

"As medium-sized Mcleod chugged a mug of home brew he yelled, 'What have you done now? Nobody told you to move my stuff! It's only your first summer pushing tin, President Jaxton. You gettin' us overnight stays with your Uncle Henry don't mean anything when it comes to who's the boss, you hear?'

"The boys was just tryin' to straighten Mcleod's messy wagon before travelin' home.

"Rags was everywhere, and they needed room fer their feet. They thought they was doin' him a favor, but Mcleod liked the clutter.

"Yep, those five added to the clankin,' and the pollution. The summer before Andrew Jaxton got hired, Mcleod had camped alone in the woods on Tama Road. Fred and John remembered seein' his wagon. Now that Andy also sold tin, the two peddlers was to meet at least once in route as kind of a trainin' program fer The President and to even up their stock. This trip, no wagons was parked in the woods, 'cause, like I said, the two stayed at Andrew Jaxton's Uncle's. Uncle Henry and his family lived on a north-south road intersectin' Tama, gist to the east of Fred and Kate's and John and Sarah's.

"Though conditions was crowded, boardin' with Henry, his wife, and eleven children sure did beat sleepin' in the woods. However, Mcleod didn't do crowded.

"Along with the conveniences of a roof and some home-cookin', the peddlers got comrades. The two tinners and short Absalom was in their early twenties, and Jake was close to eighteen, but could pass fer older 'cause of his height and good looks.

"Mcleod's presence made them hard to miss at the railroad election. People said later the peddler didn't tolerate much questionin', least of all concernin' his whereabouts. Many wondered if he had lived in Canada. He said he hailed originally from Scottish decent. His reddish hair give him away.

"His eyes was blue. Other'n them traits he had a somewhat regular appearance fer a twenty-three-year-old, 'cept he hardly ever smiled.

"Earlier on Saturday, when the peddler stopped, Sarah noticed him watch Mary. Without even seein' the merchandise, Sarah said, 'I'll take two pie tins, and three cups.' She bought 'em quick gist to git rid of him. 'Goes to show yuh, there's somethin' about a woman's intuition.

"At Fred's, Kate offered him fresh-baked cookies. He replied, 'I don't like molasses.'

"Hearin' a slight edge to his voice, Kate wanted to add, 'And I don't like tin.' But she held her tongue and bought a cup fer baby Emma. Like Sarah, she made her purchase and quickly sent him on his way.

"Thinkin' back, Kate thought somethin' in the peddler's tone implied 'she shoulda know'd he didn't like molasses,' or maybe inferred she didn't meet his high standards fer a customer, cause it wasn't modern to use molasses instead of sugar. Perhaps he'd insinuated, 'Only poor people buy gist one tin cup.'

"He reminded her of a child who didn't know how to play well with others. Most of what he told her was about 'me and mine.' No questions was asked about them and theirs.

"Some said when the peddler got skunk drunk at the railroad 'lection, he rambled on concernin' his bossy mother. Her take on the scriptures sounded more like 'Love is impatient and unkind and insists on its own way' than the 'patient and kind' version. He told, 'She gave me food and shelter. She expected I'd be like the famous preacher I was named after. It didn't matter whether I did or didn't resemble him, she screamed at me just the same.'

"Yuh know, Tom, there's a reason why 'patient' comes before 'kind.' People won't never be truly kind when they's already impatient.

"Onlookers said Mcleod almost did an oratory tellin' the details of his life, but not in a straight line. It made him hard to follow. It was the others who had to be patient while he pushed his way through his story, all about him. He bragged, 'I can butcher. I cut the heads off chickens when I was four. I practiced on kittens.'

'The potato famine drove my ma's family from their country. She had to wait a month to board a coffin ship, pushing her trip over into late summer and hurricane season. The boat was overcrowded, and full of rats, and roaches. Toilets averaged one per hundred. Even a blind man could tell when a coffin ship landed from the smell of death.'

"The people who heard Mcleod spoutin' off said it was like he was braggin' and enjoyed sayin' the bad. He would lick his lips. Sometimes he clapped his hands when he finished, like he was applaudin' himself. They didn't remember the peddler tellin' of one happy moment.

"When he wasn't bemoanin' his family, he found another complaint. Nothin' was good enough, and nothin' was good for Alexander Mcleod. It was like he'd sunk in a field of black muck.

"Mcleod said, 'The ship made the women cook their own food. My ma and grandma had to fight their way into the ship's kitchen. She wasn't scared to slug anyone. The kitchen measured six by twelve feet—about the same size as my peddler wagon. When lucky, they got one meal a day.'

"He told it like no one else had ever experienced anythin' so awful, and, like he, fer sure, had the saddest story making him some kind of star in the 'my life is so difficult' contest, like bein' seen a victim was what was most important to him.

"He said the sleepin' quarters on the ship was four tiers high and about eighteen inches wide. Sometimes two slept in one bunk, snorin' with complete strangers, men mixed with women.

"The way the peddler told it, some figured his ma mighta got raped.

"After he glorified her fer survivin' such hardship, Mcleod dropped her like a hot coal. Imbibin' more whiskey, he told how he hated her bossin'and questionin', but when she concocted the idea of him bein' a salesman and peddlin' tin, he was mighty excited. I'm guessin' it was his big chance to git away to escape her clawin' remarks. He said, 'My father was hen-pecked and kowtowed to her controllin' questions of why…what…where…when…who…and how. I'll never be done-in by any woman.'

"You know, Tom, you gist can't trust a person who'll turn on his own flesh and blood."

Tom nodded.

"Yep, Mcleod was one heck of a huckster. Stayin' at Uncle Henry's offered him a chance to try out his mum's bossy ways on short Absalom, who, everyone knew, 'wasn't quite right.' The community referred to the boy as 'slow,' and some used worse words. With his oily blond hair most never combed and stickin' up like it did, Abs resembled a short wildman. He didn't bathe much. Most people avoided him.

"Absalom craved attention so he didn't mind havin' the peddler tell him what to do. Mcleod ordered him around, sayin' stuff like, 'I left my hat on my wagon. Go get it. While you're there, crawl under to check on the back spring. I think it might have a rock in it. My horses need water. Give 'em two five-gallon buckets full.'

"Fer Absalom bein' bossed was better 'n no notice at all. It certainly ranked higher 'n havin' people walk the other way. In the beginnin', Abs followed every command.

"At eighteen, Jake was the baby in this cluster of grapes, but at home, he was in the middle of a stretch of three boys close in age. The offspring went Absalom, Jake, and then, with no girls in between to mellow 'em out, came young George.

"Havin' followed Absalom in birth order, Jake gist wanted to be normal. Younger, and as I said, much taller, Jake was eye-strikin' with his shiny black hair and eyes to match and the height. In spite of bein' quiet, he wasn't anywheres near dumb. Still waters run deep, yuh know."

Tom wasn't sure if Phil expected a reply. He guessed, probably not. Once again, he shook his head in agreement and continued scrubbing.

"In Jake's efforts to be opposite of Abs, Jake came to be a people pleaser, which kin be both an asset and a curse. When decisions is small, and the other guy's honest, people pleasin' kin work out gist fine…like cooperation or bein' a good boy or girl. However, people-pleasers kin forgit to use their own minds altogether, becomin' bystanders to the works of…well, the devil himself.

"Like Absalom, Jake beamed when Cousin Andy and Mcleod included him in their drinkin' adventures. The railroad 'lection rated as the best event so far. Everyone thought the booze got siphoned Saturday night, but the other reason Jake had for tidying the peddler's wagon was he found a place to stash a small flask. Liquor numbed the pain of bein' a follower.

"George, the youngest of the three, resented gettin' left out. 'Cause of recent trouble with the law fer assaultin' an elderly man, Henry was careful not to risk another offence. Henry decided George's age might raise a red flag if he was allowed some 'lection brew, and George couldn't vote anyway.

"Now, let me tell yuh about Henry's nephew, the other peddler, Andrew Jaxton. Andy's family lived on a plank road close to Huntington, Indiana. The road was relatively new with the main thoroughfare reachin' all the way down to within ten miles or so of Uncle Henry's. Andrew's dad was a doctor. Yep, his parents had named him after President Andrew Jackson, however, his middle name was spelled 'J- a- x- t- o- n.'

"Andrew suffered from a condition called neuralgia. Sometimes he got migraines. He had sciatica, too. Bein' a peddler allowed him time off when he was hurtin', but ridin' in a huckster wagon didn't do much fer soothin' his condition.

"This drinkin' party, minus George, returned late Saturday night from the 'lection, soaked with sights, sounds, and scents, and, well, gist plain soaked."

CHAPTER 6 — SUNDAY, JUNE 23, 1872

A quick sniff differentiates good from rotten.

Tom had scrubbed about an eighth of the way across the ceiling. Having blackened even more than the walls, this job would take longer than he had anticipated. He told Phil, "I'll be right back after I dump this water, and then you can tell me more."

Phil closed his eyes to think about what happened next. It would be the hardest part for him to tell. He hoped he wouldn't set to cryin'.

When Tom returned, he thought he saw Phil's eyes glisten. The young janitor wondered if he'd inadvertently left some soap on his glasses, and the sting had caused the old man to tear up.

Phil put down his spectacles and resumed his tale. "I'm gonna tell how it was come Sunday mornin'. The folks on

Tama Road most all headed to church. Three houses of worship had been built on a five mile stretch of the road—two to the west, one to the east. Everyone but three from Henry's house went east to Liberty Chapel. It was a Quaker Church. Fred and Kate went to a reformed log cabin one close to town. I'm not sure where John and Sarah went. John was church-shy after the Civil War. It was hard to equate a lovin' God with what he'd seen.

"With thirteen regularly occupyin' Henry's dwellin', and two peddlers uppin' the number to fifteen, minus those who stayed home, a dozen traveled south and around the corner to Liberty Chapel. Uncle Henry, George, and Cousin Andy was the ones who stayed home. Even Alexander Mcleod, with his blood-shot eyes, showed up at Sunday service.

"No logical reason existed fer young George not goin,' except maybe he was too jittery to sit still fer much prayer. The main reason he give later was he hoped he would finally have Cousin Andy to himself. But Cousin Andy was sleepin' somethin' off…either the railroad election or a migraine, or both.

"Andy said, 'My neuralgia's acting up.'

"George noticed the odor of the 'lection preceded and followed every word Andrew spoke. Either condition coulda give him a bad headache. Old Henry showed similar symptoms. George figured, *Andy's migraine's been pickled, and Dad's just pickled.*

"Henry and Andy showed their faces gist long enough to see the corn and toss their cookies at the edge of the field. They set on the porch fer a bit to recoup from their efforts. George heard his dad say, 'Well I'll be horn-swallowed. Look who's comin!' They was shocked to see Abs and Mcleod around 11:30, when the usual time would have been noon.

"George was encouraged. Maybe he'd git included in some fun. The remainin' ten arrived about a half hour later, as expected. Henry questioned why the two come so early. Mcleod answered, 'I didn't like sitting with my eyes closed.' Without warnin', Mcleod, Absalom, and Jake left again. Before they departed, George overheard Mcleod ask Jake, 'Did you see any girls from church come this way?'

"Immediately after they'd gone, Henry complained, 'The sun's way too bright this mornin'.' Both Henry and Andy took their cue to depart as well. They meandered back up the stairs into the darkened bedrooms. George remembered hearin' his pa speak as they left, 'Though we didn't go to service, we did a great service by drainin' those jugs of wheat wine in time for this year's harvest.'

"George found himself alone again. He seethed and sulked. He understood the reason why he couldn't go to the railroad 'lection, but not why he wasn't bein' included in the search fer some girls.

"George watched Mcleod, Jake, and Absalom run across the road and into the woods. Abs had trouble keepin' up. They appeared to be headin' toward Tama Road. It was an easy sprint on a well-worn deer path, about a mile and a half or there abouts. Even if Abs got way behind, he wouldn't git lost."

"Though the Sitterleys didn't go to Liberty Church, they still let Mary attend with Grandpa, Elias, and Marion. She needed the security, and it was, as I said, a Quaker congregation with rituals different from their own.

"On Sunday mornin', after she'd eaten her sweet roll, Mary mentioned her horrible nightmare. She said, 'I'd been caught and hurt, maybe even killed, in the dream.' John said, 'Go look in the mirror, Belle. It was just a dream. You don't have a single scratch on your pretty face.'

"Mary donned her pink dress and her brand-new bonnet with the special green ribbons. She grabbed her parasol and her Testament. It took about an hour for the walk to Liberty Chapel. On the way, she stopped by her grandparents'. Grandpa Strouse had been waitin' for her. As they traveled the uneven dirt road, Mary told him about a goose-bump feelin', like she'd returned to her bad dream.

"Mary said, 'It happened right here on Tama Road. I was headed home. Fog hovered over the fields, like we saw early this morning. I saw an angel. She tried to warn me before I was brutally attacked!'

"Grandpa Strouse recalled how Mary choked up. 'My only comfort is then my dream shifted. I fell and hit the ground hard beside Mama's grave. I tried to move but couldn't. I woke up with cold chills. I wasn't sure if I was dead or alive, but I think I was dead!'

"Grandpa Strouse said Mary looked like she was about to cry. Tryin' his best to console her, he said, 'It must'a been somethin' you ate, Mary. Happens to me all the time. How much raspberry pie did you have yesterday?'

"Mary laughed. Maybe she had eaten more than her share."

"On Sunday, Mary didn't have to make decisions, and life didn't change. Each family always sat in the same pew. It soothed Mary to have this place. At Friends' Church, they would pray for a long time, 'til someone might speak or shake hands with the person next to them, startin' the process fer everyone. Sunday School was different. She learned about their beliefs, and folks was allowed to talk.

"Usually no new faces attended Quaker Meetings. That mornin', however, Mcleod sat in a pew near the front. About midway through, he and Abs left. Mary forgot and whispered to Grandpa, 'No one ever leaves church early unless they are sick. Those two don't look ill.'

"In church school, they did the usual readin' of Psalms and somethin' from the New Testament. She hurried to find the texts. Mary had learned all the books in the Bible. It became a game for her to see how fast she could find 'em. She'd memorized 'em in groups of three or four. Some was easy like 'Joshua Judges Ruth.' 'Galatians, Ephesians, and Philippians' seemed to flow, but she forgot what come next and without the first, the followin' two was completely gone. Mary told her friends, 'Maybe our teacher forgets, too, 'cause he hardly ever gets beyond Philippians.'

"One of the parishioners collected an offering. She loved watchin' him twirl the empty basket a couple of times and smile before he passed it through. Mary told her friends, 'I'm surprised they let him have so much fun in church.'

"The Sitterleys handed her a coin fer the offering. Grandpa Strouse had given her one, too. Her friends saw her drop 'em in slowly, one at a time from kind of high above the plate.

"A few of the ornery boys brought clay marbles and bowled 'em down the slanted wooden floor."

37

Remembering some of his own antics, Tom grinned.

"Church School was first. It was durin' the meeting, however, Mary's serious work began. She knew she must stay alert during prayer, 'cause Grandpa Strouse sometimes fell asleep. The noddin' off wasn't the problem. The difficulty was Strouse snored louder'n anyone in the whole congregation. From about the age of three, Mary's mama taught her to nudge him if he showed any signs of suckin' in air like people do before they let out a loud exhale. It was her mama's job as a little girl, too.

"Mary became good at readin' the signals. First, his hands dropped. His chin followed suit, slowly droopin' to his chest. The chin lowerin' occurred in small increments, after which, he'd begin suckin' in air as his lower jaw slowly lifted again in them same small shifts. Then, right before he let out a sound, Mary would poke him with her elbow. Grandpa would jerk his head, open his eyes wide, and pretend to be at prayer. Stiflin' her giggles, Mary would squint her eyes tight, and bite her lower lip to keep from laughin'. She told her friends she guessed this was why they sat in the back pew.

"Followin' church, she got to see Marion and some of her friends. After they departed, she and Grandpa headed west to his house. Grandpa asked, 'How about staying for dinner?'

"He remembered Mary's exact words, 'Not today, Grandpa. Sarah has raspberry pie.'

"Smilin' at the reminder of his tease, Grandpa winked. As he watched her turn to go, Grandpa Strouse considered Belle's dream. The memory caused him to stand by the road for a long time, and keep his eyes fixed on her until she completely disappeared from his sight.

CHAPTER 7 — GEORGE'S WATCH

It was the kind of day you see death etched in the fallen bark of trees as if nature is determined to remind us.

Tom needed a breather. He leaned against his stepladder. He figured he'd hear footsteps come down the hall soon enough for him to look busy since nearly every board in the infirmary floor creaked as much or more than its residents.

Phil said, "Piece by piece this disaster unfolded. I know it's takin' kinda long to build, but the situation eventually popped out gist like a jack-in-the-box. All stuffed and stored in, it sprung out full-force and exploded right in front of us like one of the dirty bubbles in your bucket.

"Back at Uncle Henry's, George fidgeted as he waited fer Cousin Andy to recover, or the other three to return, whichever come first. He sat by the split rail fence in a shady spot and surveyed the corn blowin' in the wind. He fingered the watch and chain in his pocket. He'd received 'em fer his birthday. It was one of those years when the world seemed to be tellin' him he should keep track of time. Neither piece was of precious metal. No gold or silver lined George's pockets. He seldom got presents, but this year was special. It was the birthday when girls is called 'sweet.' The tradition in Henry's family was the males got a watch, all 'cept fer Absalom who didn't git one 'cause he couldn't tell time.

"George sulked. He rechecked the hour again and again. He held the watch close to his ear thinkin', maybe it had stopped. He wound it many times even though he could still hear it ticking. He wondered what his brothers and the tin peddler was doin' and why they'd been gone so long. No one had eaten since breakfast. His stomach growled as he grrr-ed in despair over bein' left home alone fer the whole blessed day.

"One o'clock passed. It was an undertakin' to open the timepiece, still stiff from the newness and with a small clasp. George needed fingernails to wedge under, but George didn't have ones long enough. What little might grow, the boy chewed back to the quick and sometimes beyond. He had a reputation fer bein' on the nervous side. Some of the kids from school called him 'jumpy George.'

"Three times in the last two days the tin peddler and his own brothers had deserted him. Three times he'd experienced the feelin' of bein' dumped 'cause he was too young.

"At Fred and Kate's, Kate put the children down for their naps. Anton wasn't sleepy. He snuck out of his bed and tiptoed to the window to see if 'Belle was headed their way. Then, forgittin' he wasn't doin' as he'd been told, he bolted into the main part of their cabin.

'Mama, Papa! Birds! Birds!'

"Fred left his rocker. He'd been reading, as was his habit on Sunday afternoon. Sure enough, a huge flock swooshed from the woods down a ways from their cabin sweepin' the air like giant broom bristles, same as yuh'd see right before a bad storm. Fred concluded a large animal musta ruffled their feathers. He comforted Anton sayin' 'Look at the sky, Anton. I don't see storm clouds, do you?' Anton shook his head.

"Kate said, 'Whatever spooked the birds isn't going to hurt you, Anton. Go back to bed. If you want Mary to come later this afternoon, you must take your nap now.'

"Fred went back to readin'. Kate picked up her sampler, which she didn't consider work, but pleasure.

"Around 1:30, when George rechecked his watch, he heard the familiar squeak of their pump handle followed by a gush of water. Lookin' toward the barn, he spotted Absalom hard at work doin' the crankin' while Mcleod washed. He saw Jake hasten into the house alone.

"George couldn't help but notice the bright red stains on Mcleod's shirt. Mcleod scrubbed at the ones on his wrist with the first water flowin' out of the pump. The pump was made of iron. No pot on the stove coulda heated liquid any better.

"George yelled, 'Hey, Alex, don't you know only cold water removes blood?'

"Mcleod had set them stains. Then, strange as it was, the peddler put another shirt, a striped one, right over top of the tainted one. George wondered why Mcleod didn't remove the soggy one first and hang it to dry. They had a clothesline in front of their house. If worried about forgettin' it, he coulda hung it on one of the hooks on his wagon.

"George ran to the pump. 'What the heck happened to you, Alex?'

"The red-haired, red-faced peddler snapped back, 'Can't you tell, Gee-oorge? I had a nosebleed'!"

CHAPTER 8 — MONDAY, JUNE 24, 1872

The sunrise was bright, clear, and strikingly orange. Cornstalk metronomes swayed their leafy pendulums in the early morning breeze. Fields of grain paced the time from birth to death. Wound by the wind, the stately green stalks softly ticked, "hush, hush, hush.

Knowing he needed to get back to work, Tom moved the ladder. He balanced his cleaning bucket on the support.

Old Phil continued with a sigh. "Things seemed normal. Early Monday mornin', Sarah Sitterley opened her eyes. Any farm wife worth her salt knew it was 'warsh' day. I always wondered if the 'r' in 'warsh' helped clean the memory of war outta their lives, sort of like 'war. . .shhhhhhhh.' They was less than ten years out from the Civil one, yuh know.

"Mary had called the Sitterley house 'home' fer three years. John and Sarah was so pleased with her, they'd made her the heir to their estate.

'Their thirteen-year-old heiress weren't home yet. Sarah figured she'd spent the night with her grandparents as often happened on Sundays. Sarah wanted to have the cows milked and laundry hung by the time Belle returned. She guessed Mary's pink dress wouldn't be so mussed, it would need launderin'. Mary was careful with her clothin', 'specially her favorites.

"Sarah loved buyin' pretty clothes fer the girl. She 'specially liked the new bonnet with the wide ribbons. She said she thought it was 'the perfect finishing touch.' She had Mary tie them offside, instead of in the middle of her chin. It was 'more fashionable.'

"Doin' laundry was a complex task. Mrs. Sitterley brought in small pieces of wood and built a fire in the cook stove. She situated the copper boiler and filled it with the water she'd carried into their summer kitchen.

"Sarah'd recently made new batches of soap usin' lard from the hogs butchered in the early spring. Yuh know, Tom, everythin' got used but the squeal.

"Makin' soap was dangerous 'cause of the lye and the hot, spattery lard, but Sarah's mother taught her how, and her soap was always as white as snow. Some people used old lard or bacon grease and got a rancid smellin' soap with a rusty brown color. It never made Sarah feel clean. It didn't seem

45

wasteful to her to use fresh lard. The soap would be fer bathin', laundry, and all cleanin' chores, includin' the dishes. It was the only soap they owned. Some items was store-bought, but not her soap. Sarah loved its whiteness, 'so pure, so new.' Sarah sang a little ditty about lye soap, not always in tune, but the song in her heart was in perfect pitch.

"Once the laundry was done, she planned on bakin' a fresh raspberry pie in the new tins she bought from the peddler. I'm tellin' you all this, so as yuh'll know what Sarah was like. She was careful 'bout most everythin' she done."

"Around six a.m. on this same Monday mornin', early as it was, Mcleod and Andy had already harnessed their horses. Mcleod had determined they'd leave as soon as it got light. He jumped onto his wagon. Jake joined him.

"Mcleod screamed, 'Get the lead out, Absalom! We're waiting on you'."

"Absalom's short legs lumbered his awkward body onto Andy's wagon, but Andy didn't know why he had a passenger. Instead of headin' north and back to Ft. Wayne, Mcleod headed south. At the first crossroad, he turned to the right onto Tama Road. At the east edge of the big woods, he jerked his team to a stop. He halted so sudden, The President had to pull back on his horses to avoid a collision.

Andy wondered, *If Mcleod's in such a hurry, why did he halt? As fast as he was going on this rough patch of road, maybe his harness or the wagon broke, or likely his horse turned lame.*

"Andy watched Jake jump to the ground whereupon his tall cousin immediately bent to pick up a scrap of ribbon barely visible 'midst the matchin' blades of grass. It was close to a cluster of orange daylilies. President Jaxton questioned Absalom, 'Why the heck are we stopping to get a ribbon? Does Mcleod think it qualifies as a rag?'

"Absalom stared straight ahead, shivered, and didn't give an answer. Ab's face lost all its color.

"Next, Jake lifted a big chunk of rooted grass and soil. From under it, he unearthed a flask of what looked to be whiskey. He took a lengthy swig.

"Andy pondered, *I guess not all the booze got drunk at the election, but how and why did it end up here?* Andrew noticed Jake's face go ashen, too.

"With no warnin', Andy's horses bolted. He pulled back hard. They reared, and tried to take off. Strugglin' to gain control, Andy yelled to Mcleod, 'For God's sake, go on!'

"No flies or bees was botherin,' and no one or nothin' was around to startle 'em. Andrew's team was normally quite calm.

Hearin' tin rattle, and travelin' in the big city of Ft. Wayne had numbed 'em to most everythin'.

"Mcleod did move on. And Andy's horses finally settled down. Shortly, however, Mcleod stopped again, this time at Leininger's cabin to ask fer rags. Andy thought, *It's way too early to be interrupting a family's morning routine, even a farm family's*.

"Mcleod's schedule, actions, and route was makin' no sense. Again, Andy thought, *For God's sake, go on…*

CHAPTER 9—WHERE'S MARY?

The flies and mosquitoes made their rounds. Like nature's alarm clock, they awoke the men, women, and children with whom they shared a space. Attempting to ignore the irritations, the responsible rural community delved into its day.

Tom was determined to finish the ceiling by noon. Mid-day seemed a reasonable goal. Then he'd break for lunch. Because he had to move the ladder frequently, and because of the uncomfortable neck position, he figured the Infirmery's ten-foot ceiling would take as long, or longer, to complete than the four walls. Though the young janitor now wanted, he decided he couldn't stop and listen.

Phil said, "Let me tell yuh more about Mrs. Sitterley. Sarah was one to plan ahead. Not enough hours existed in a day to do everythin' a farm wife was expected to git done. Most every country woman loved the little poem, 'Man may work from sun to sun, but woman's work is never done.' 'Course they didn't say it in front of their man.

"With laundry on the line, Sarah picked the black raspberries growin' next to the woods. 'Ping, ping, ping,' she dropped them into her empty bucket. As she removed the fruit, she remembered noticin' little white ghost-cones lingerin' on the green stems under where each berry had formed. Sarah remarked later how 'the small heads centered amidst leafy green halos.'

"She recalled touchin' each dark fruit reverently like the individual bead on a rosary. Pickin' 'em was a kind of a prayer fer her.

"As she moved from one vine to the next, a thorn caught her arm. The branch moved with her and left small wounds in her skin as she separated from the briar.

"Sarah observed how growin' conditions effected the berries—some was big and beautiful, others, small. They had the same water and soil. Maybe they didn't get the same amount of sun. *Was it over- crowding?* Those cramped in any way grew tight and seedy.

"Holdin' a black-purple handful, she admired her bounty. Her skin absorbed the stain. Mosquitoes swarmed the patch and buzzed her face. A tiny green spider and a grey stink bug climbed the fruit in her bucket. They found separate routes across the berry mountain. Using a leaf, Sarah squashed the spider. With another leaf, she captured the stink bug and dropped the grey creature onto the ground. She smashed it with the heel of her shoe to keep the smell at a distance. 'Guess Sarah thought of this later 'cause of how Mary had used her footwear.

"She did some samplin', then headed home.

"This time when mixin' the crust, she left out the vinegar. She rolled a layer of dough fer the top of the pie and carved her art. While others cut leaves, vines, and circles, Sarah carved cornstalks. How everyone loved her black raspberry pie. It was definitely Mary's favorite.

"Sarah thought, *After the pie is done, maybe Mary will be home, and we can pick green beans. We have a plentiful crop. I'll be glad for the help. Their color reminds me of the ribbons on her new bonnet.*

"Sarah always formed her hair into a neat bun, but try as she might, she couldn't keep the front strands in place, 'specially when workin' over the hot stove. It curled thick and hung in pretty locks on her forehead. Once a petite girl, she'd lost the slim in her figure to the lard she cooked with and the wheat John grew in the field.

"Timein' the swish of her wooden rollin' pin with the 'hush' of the cornstalks, she sang the little ditty about lye soap, and shaped the last scraps of dough fer some rolled-up cinnamon and sugar 'bumblebees.' Nothin' was wasted."

"At Fred and Kate's, the air was full of energy, almost as full as Fred himself. Kate said his hair did an extra flip on the back of his head from the 'cessive humidity. The heat sat on 'em and refused to move.

"Fred loved to work. He was lookin' forward to a day of hard labor in the wheat field, havin' readied himself fer the past week. He saw John load his freshly sharpened scythe onto his wagon.

"The rays of the mornin' sun pierced like thousands of needles stuck round a molten pin cushion. The hot beams pierced every thread of clothin' it touched. Dogs panted under trees rather than follow their masters. Smells became smellier as the temperature rose. Fred knew anythin' at all pleasant from the early mornin' hours would pass quickly, but the steaminess didn't matter to Fred. Kate frowned about the swelterin' weather, but Fred smiled and said, 'It's makin' the corn grow.' As was his custom, he fed his animals and milked his cows, then came in to eat his own breakfast. He, Kate, and the children all ate together once morning chores was done.

"Strawberry jam sparkled red on top of the golden, fresh-churned butter Phebe had helped crank. Fred said the prayer…every day, every meal, 'the same prayer. 'God is great and God is good, and we thank Him for our food. By His hands we all are fed. Give us Lord our daily bread. Amen.'

"The word 'food' sounded more like 'fould,' in his carry-over German accent. 'Fould' does, after-all, rhyme with 'good.'

"Fred got a big boost from Katherine's breakfasts. He often remarked, 'Do I eat to live, or live to eat?' As he mopped the last trace of egg off his plate with a piece of Kate's homemade bread, he winked at her and added, 'Waste not, want not!'

"The children's smiles circled with red jam. They, too, was excited about the harvest, though still disappointed. Phebe said, 'Mary never came to see us.'

Kate replied, 'Maybe she had to stay over with her grandparents.' A quick swipe of three sticky faces and their day began.

"It wasn't nothin' ever went wrong in Fred and Kate's cabin, or no one was ever edgy, angry, or sad. Seems like the work ethic, Kate's singin', and their faith and devotion to family and friends added bricks to their lives. When life rattled or the wolf come to the door, the foundation might shake, but it didn't crumble. Cracks might break inside the mortar, but those got filled, and life went on. Fred believed no problem was so big it couldn't be solved, or at least endured.

"I'm guessin' sometimes Fred thought he still heard the ocean and smelled sauerkraut and vomit, but he put them memories aside in the German way and carried on. It was as if he was born to be responsible.

"I remember lots more he enjoyed sayin', like, 'Don't put off until tomorrow what you can do today...A stitch in time, saves nine...Love is patient and kind...Turn the other cheek.' Them words was the mortar solidifyin' his life, at least until Monday, June twenty-fourth, when the foundations on Tama Road crumbled like they'd been hit by a tornado.

"Fred hitched his team and loaded his scythe onto the wagon. He waved at John.

"Fred had trained his horses so well, he never had to raise his voice to 'em. It gist took the soft click of the lines and Fred's tongue and Babe and Baldy moved steadily forward. 'No one ever saw him lay a hand on 'em, even at pullin' contests, when most others was yellin' and whippin' theirs. Fred had this knack with both animals and people.

"Meanwhile, Kate's kitchen harbored some catastrophes. Baby Emma, who was learnin' to sit, fell forward and hit her head on the table. It was a bruise and some tears. Little Anton tried to eat as much as his daddy and said, 'I have tummy ache.' Kate put a wet cloth on Emma, and then picked mint and made tea fer Anton.

"She started the laundry, cautionin' the children about the hot stove, as if anyone would want to get close to somethin' hotter than the air. The children played on the floor with rag dolls and the small wagon Fred had made Anton fer Christmas.

"Life was simple but complex. The work was hard 'cause it counted so much on human strength. Tools and machines was nothin' compared to now. Toys was few and un-demanded. Fer the most part children found ways to entertain themselves. Phebe and Anton played hide and seek with each other and peek with Baby Emma. On rainy days, they played "hide the thimble," though somedays Kate held her breath about ever finding it again when Anton forgot where he'd put it. The important information about 'seek and you will find' was in the children's games.

"Kate was strong. Work and childbearin' went well fer her. She had the laundry ready to hang by eight. She gathered the basket and the children, and they all went to the backyard clothesline. She propped the center with the wooden post Fred had cut into a V fer support. She began to string the laundry.

"Yuh know, Tom, tellin' every detail gits more and more important when life's slammed against death. It's amazin' how much becomes sacred.

Tom nodded and looked Phil's way, but once again the old man gave him no time to reply, not that he could have anyway.

"Kate sang her mornin' songs. She had this beautiful voice. It was clear and clean like her laundry and the early air. She paused to take breaths between the phrases as she bent to grab another item. Had it been rainin', she would have hung the garments in their small cabin. Monday was, after all, 'warsh' day.

"She continued her melodies. 'Bringing in the sheaves, bringing in the sheaves, we shall come rejoicing, bringing in the the sheaves…' She found singin' and bein' outside soothed the children. It was like they melted right into the grass, and the closer they was to it, the more at peace they got. Sticks and stones, and the dirt itself became their toys. They found leaves and bugs and flowers. They spent allota time huntin' pill bugs, some people calls 'em 'rolly pollies,' and watchin' 'em turn into little balls when uncovered from under a rock.

"The children sang along with their mama, 'specially Phebe, who by now knew most of the words. As if on cue, when the singin' stopped, Great Grandma came out of the house next door. The white hairs on her head was sparse with age, and her pink skin showed through, reflectin' the sunshine, but still she pulled her fragile hair back into a tight bun. Her dress was of a dark material and hung to the ground since she was bent with age and from the labor of life. Grandma's posture made the dress look about four inches longer in the front than the back.

Great Grandma lived with Kate's folks. She was widowed. Mostly, she sat. Her work now was to attend to the children. Sometimes Great Grandma brought cookies."

As if he'd just reminded himself, Phil located a big sugar cookie he'd saved. He took a sizeable bite leaving a congregation of crumbs on his whiskered chin. He followed with an equally large drink of water. He didn't worry about spoiling lunch. The snack spurred him on.

Phil swallowed hard, then continued: "Great Grandma waited while Kate packed vittles fer the men in the field. Like all the other wives, Kate would take food back to the farmers. No one stopped the harvest to come inside and eat. It was a great arrangement to have family next door. Grandparents came when needed." Phil added wistfully, "The elderly was still useful."

"Back at the Sitterleys, John stood knee deep in wheat. While Sarah had a lot of plans, John had only one, the harvest. First, he'd scythe the field with the grain cradle attached to keep the stems from scatterin'. The helpers would tie the bundles together into shocks. Later they'd thrash to separate the grain. They used the leftover straw mostly fer beddin' their animals, but, if needed, many families sewed straw ticks fer sleepin' on. Not the Sitterleys. They had feather ticks.

"What a dirty job wheat harvest was. It left dust floatin' in the fields and dirt whiskers over the real whiskers on the men's faces. Maybe wash day shoulda been relocated to the end of the week, but fer women, Saturdays was bakin' and goin' to town days, and Sundays was fer church, family, and rest. I always figured some kinda link existed between cleanin' the body on Saturday night, cleanin' the soul on Sunday, and washin' the clothes coverin' the body and soul on Monday. Three days out of seven, people knew gist what to do with their lives. Yep, six days a week they worked from sunrise to sunset. In a world based so strong on the need fer survival, somethin' had to be predictable.

"As the clock ticked, Sarah's uneasiness built. The chimes rang ten. Mary still wasn't home. Sarah got the key and wound their noisy mantel piece. It was fancy and loud. This was as close as she could come to fixin' time.

"Sarah peered down the road but didn't see any sign of Belle. Like Kate, she began to assemble food to carry to the field. Because John had no sons, he'd hired extra men to help with harvest. Sarah sliced meat from the ham they'd cured. She took homemade bread. She pulled and cleaned fresh carrots. She'd wait to pick the first green beans 'til Mary got home.

Smilin' over the thought, Sarah noted, *I love that the blossoms are so delicate. Sometimes they fall during picking. One has to be careful.*

"Yuh know, Tom, like I said, it's strange how every detail before and after a calamity grows so big in people's minds.

"Fer dessert, Sarah took some of the raspberry pie in the new tin. The smell made her hungry, but she'd wait to eat with the farmers. As she cut the pie, Sarah noticed how the dark purple filling had thickened gist right and wouldn't drip stickiness over the hands of the laborers. She was glad they could take a piece and eat it without need for a plate or fork. She thanked God fer the small blessin' of less she'd have to carry.

"She pumped fresh water into a brown crockery jug fer 'em to drink. She wet some clean washcloths so they could 'warsh up' before eatin'. Rememberin' the blackness of their faces and hands, she grabbed a piece of lye soap, hopin' they'd choose to scrub before grabbin' the sweet pie.

"As she crossed the field, Sarah carefully maneuvered the cut stems of wheat. Even though her socks and shoes come up high on her ankles, and her skirts come down low, stubbles poked her legs, scrapin' her berry-picking wounds, and leavin' webs of tiny red scratches. She wished fer Mary's help.

"The heat from the summer sun scathed her skin more than the heat from her kitchen stove. It blasted its sultry flames across her face. Although she wore her everyday feed-sack bonnet with the wide brim, she couldn't escape its scorch. Rays reflected from the yellow straw and double-dosed her from below as well as above. She was the fillin' in this earth-sky sandwich, gettin' fried one step at a time.

"The humidity added its scourge to the almost unbearable weather. Sweat clung to her skin and rained its salty drops down the small of her back. Sarah said how she'd thought, *Pigs don't sweat. It's why they wallow in mud puddles and die in this heat. I'm so glad I can sweat…it's keeping me alive.* Sarah was good at bein' grateful but wished later she'd forgotten about the habits of pigs.

"With each step, as if to remind herself, she repeated, 'I'm so glad I'm perspiring. I'm so glad I'm perspiring…' The chant kept her goin'. Flies, mosquitoes and an occasional gnat found her. She heard their buzzin', and felt them land, but had no free hands to swat 'em away. She shook 'em off as best she could. One pesky fly never left. It followed her clear 'cross the field.

"The smell of rodents blended with the odor of ripened grain. A mouse scurried at her feet. She saw a black snake slither not far behind.

"As Sarah struggled with her load, she rehearsed how she'd tell John of her concern about Mary's delayed arrival. She knew he wouldn't want to leave the field 'til he was done. She decided she would have to determine what to do if Mary wasn't home when she returned.

"Sarah had left a sandwich, carrots, and a big piece of raspberry pie on the table. She'd writ a note in English on Mary's school slate and placed it next to the food. It read, 'Dear Mary, I hope you like the pie. There's no vinegar. Love, Sarah.'

"Sarah never did sign her name 'Mama,' or ask Mary to call her any form of the word. She knew she'd not replace Susannah. Yet, she hoped someday Belle might decide to use this special term of endearment.

"As she neared the workers, John looked up from his scythe. Sarah thought, *They'll soon have the first field ready to thrash.* She hurried as fast as she could.

"In addition to the pie tins, Sarah Sitterley had bought tin cups from Mcleod. Tin didn't wear out, but it did get dented and disfigured, somehow matchin' her feelin's about the peddler. She didn't want damaged cups to tip on uneven ground and spill the water. Refills didn't come easy with the pump so far away. I'm bettin' yuh understand, don't yuh, Tom?"

61

This time Tom replied, "Yep, sure do." He hoped old Phil would quit talking about carrying water. Though Phil repeated himself from time to time, Tom tolerated it because of Phil's age. All in all, Phil was doing a decent job of telling the story. For sure, he wasn't leaving much out.

"Sensin' a change, Sarah glanced at the sky. A few clouds pointed their massive fingers high into what had been a blue-sky day. Sarah noticed a white belt formin'. She said it separated heaven and earth as if the earth was wearing a corset. Sarah claimed, 'It made the sky look like a big blue dome cushioned by clouds on a giant platter of green and grain.'

"Sarah called out, 'John!' His first response surprised her. Instead of sayin', 'Hey men, it's chow time,' he said, 'Where's Belle?'

'She's not home yet. I'm worried.'

'She's probably helping her grandfolks.'

"While Sarah dispensed food and water, John and his hired help chatted about what happened last week gist across the state line. John asked, 'Did you hear how a team of horses got hit by lightning? It killed the team outright and melted the pattern of the harness into the horses' hides.'

'I heard it was a team of Normans.'

'They say the farmer was also struck.'

'Someone said he hasn't been right since.'

'At least he survived. Maybe he'll come out of it, though I heard it killed his son'."

"John quickly changed the subject. It was an unwritten rule in the Sitterley household...one didn't dwell on negative thoughts. Gratitude was their treatment fer narrow escapes and pain. They favored the sayin', 'There's always somethin' to be thankful for,' emphasizin' the words 'somethin' and 'thankful.' But John couldn't come up with anythin' over the loss of a son.

"The weather, even when bad, was a safe subject. It was what it was, and as fer as anyone knew, was beyond human control. John remarked, 'I see clouds rising. I hope a storm isn't brewing. Let's count the shocks while Sarah finishes handing out lunch.'

"One counted a hundred and ten, one a hundred and nine, and one didn't know how to count, but he was a good worker.

"John warshed the black from his hands and face and became recognizable. Conversation ceased. The only time they didn't pray out loud before eatin' was in the field. Sarah thought, *Somehow, praying out loud only goes with sitting.* Standin' in the hot field, she said her quiet prayer of gratitude fer what was good. From deep inside, though, another thought come to her, *You just don't thank God for evil.*

"Sarah said she give this silent prayer. *Thank You for getting me across the wheat field without tripping and dumping the food and water. I'm so glad the oats bugs are mostly in the fields. Only a few have found the raspberries. We're grateful for a fine harvest. Thanks for helping John and the other farmers finish before it rains. Thank You that Mary will be home soon.* Sarah said this prayer with her eyes wide open but told later how she forgot to say 'amen.'

"Yep, Sarah was determined to find ways to be grateful. Havin' been childless fer so long taught her this survival skill. It was her favorite tool. She said it guided her spirit to keep it alive. She believed gratitude opens the door to miracles.

"She'd learned early on how being sad or angry or bitter doesn't make life any better. She'd heard at church about how gratitude and grace came from the same word. It was Greek or Roman or Hebrew or somethin'. It made sense to Sarah, 'g-r-a' fer gra-teful gra-ce. She 'picked it in large bouquets' when she needed to refresh dismal thoughts. She clung tight to her bywords, 'I'm so glad.' Seldom did she go through a day without sayin' those words. She also often said, 'Add a little extra.' A good attitude's what kept her goin'.

"With the men well fed, and the sky gradually darkenin' with the threat of incomin' rain, the air sat on 'em gist like it did all of Tama Road. It seemed to have no intention of movin' into even the slightest breeze. Gist after they'd eaten, however, the wind picked up with every indication of a storm.

"Sarah hurried home. Still no Mary. She debated hitchin' the buggy horse, but thinkin' how long it would take, she figured she could walk it gist as fast. Surely she could beat an incomin' rain. If not, a soakin' might feel real good. She'd forgotten about the Norman horses.

"Sarah quickly headed east. The buggies and wagons had channeled uneven paths durin' spring downpours. Country roads was narrow. You couldn't pass. Someone had to pull offside and wait. She walked in the grass and weeds, thinkin' it easier than tryin' to maneuver the ruts. Tama Road was made of dirt. Life was messy.

"Passin' the smell of Wienman's hogs, Sarah thought again about how pigs couldn't take the heat, and how they wallow in mud to try to keep cool. Once more, she determined to be glad she could sweat. As she neared Strouse's, she hoped to see Mary somewhere in the yard, maybe snappin' green beans under the big shade tree. She saw no one. Surely they wouldn't have decided to hitch the wagon and head into town. Normally no one goes on a Monday, but people sometimes act strange as they age. Maybe Grandma Strouse had taken ill, and they went for a doctor.

"Purple berry stains were still on Sarah's fingers when she knocked on Strouse's door. She saw him move slowly through the house. She didn't see Mary.

"When he greeted her, she didn't greet him back. Instead she questioned, 'Where's Mary?'

"Grandpa's eyes widened. In a panic of disbelief, he asked what Sarah had feared hearin'. 'She didn't come home?'

"Strouse and Sarah hitched the horse as fast as they could and drove as quick as the ruts would allow. Grandpa Strouse told Sarah, 'Mary left my house right after church and headed for your place. After hearin' about her dream, I watched her most of the way.' Sarah's heart sank.

"John heard 'em comin'. Not seein' Mary, he dropped his work, and ran through the wheat stubble, dodgin' the shocks as he went. He grabbed Strouse's drivin' horse, unhitched it, leavin' the carriage smack-dab in the middle of the road. Grandpa and Sarah pulled the buggy into the lane as John galloped away, bareback and bridle-less.

"Hearin' John's call fer help, Fred and all the other farmers on Tama Road stopped their work to organize a search party.

CHAPTER 10 — MONDAY AFTERNOON

Afternoon songs softened into naptime lullabies. Little minds heard the singing even after it ceased. The melodies soothed tiny hearts into peaceful slumber.

Tom moved the ladder and stepped onto the first rung for his assent. However, Phil altered his custodian's plans when he said, "Let me get to what happened next, Tom, but I'm not sure you should be up on no ladder when yuh hear it.

"I'll start at Fred and Kate's. After Kate'd sung her babies to sleep, she butchered a chicken to fry. The freshly killed bird popped and spattered in the bubblin' lard. She peeled and boiled potatoes fer the evenin' meal. She'd planned to crisp them in the chicken grease when it was time to eat. Meanwhile, she'd keep the food cool in the pit in the ground where they cooled their milk. Someday she hoped to have an ice box like Sarah's.

"Advance preparation was Kate's secret. She had made an extra pie crust. The cows had given a lot of milk. She made a butterscotch filling. Kate always made an extra crust or two to help her cookin' process go faster. Along with Sarah, she believed in plannin' ahead. Kate's philosophy was, 'It wasn't rainin' when Noah built the ark.'

"With the children sound asleep, Kate could be outside alone. Quickly, she pulled the clothes off the line. She liked bringin' the garments to her nose fer a whiff of the fresh smell. 'It's as if the outside comes inside with the laundry,' she would say. Her round face reddened in the summer sun. She pulled and folded. She wiped the sweat from her forehead with her apron. Her songs slowed but was no less reassurin', 'Rescue the perishing, care for the dying, wrap them in pity from sin and the grave...Down in the human heart, Crushed by the tempter, Feelings lie buried that grace can restore; Touched by a loving heart, Wakened by kindness, Chords that were broken will vibrate once more...'

"It was at this moment when she heard John Sitterley ride by at breakneck speed, callin' fer help. She saw Fred drop his work in the field. Her heart rate quickened. Somethin' bad had happened. Maybe a team of horses ran away. She hoped Grandpa Strouse hadn't collapsed with a heat stroke, even though he normally no longer worked the field.

"What Kate didn't know was they was in fer an encounter with 'live spelled backwards.' It was a grapplin' which would never dry or fold gist right, and fer sure couldn't be hung straight on any line even with the strongest support. Instead, it would remain damp, develop a mold, and drag its stench through many generations.

"Fred brought his work horses into the barn, quickly watered them and yelled, 'Mary's missing.'

"After movin' in with the Sitterleys, Mary had often spent time at Fred and Kate's. She loved playin' with their babies. She was like an older cousin. Sometimes she helped Kate with her work, and they sang together.

"How could this be? Where would Mary have gone? What could possibly have happened between Grandpa Strouse's and home?

"Kate wasn't prone to cry much, but unbidden tears rolled down her cheeks. A feelin' of stiffness climbed her body. Fer the first time all day, Kate didn't move. She stared straight ahead.

"Surprisin'ly the children didn't wake with all the commotion, allowin' Kate to run across the yard and tell the rest of her family. She asked Great Grandma to return in case they needed her.

'Maybe Mary strayed off the path and fell. I'll bet she's waiting somewhere for us to find her,' she told Great Grandma.

"Kate tried to be reassurin', but inside she was thinkin', *What's next for this family? Wasn't it enough they were torn apart by Susannah's death?* Susannah had been Kate's friend. Three years had passed, but Kate still missed her. She had always felt God didn't give people more'n they could handle, but now she weren't so sure. A bad feelin' ripped through the pit of her stomach. *John and Sarah! Finally they had a child.*

The search committee entered the woods on Tama Road, cooler, but darker and more difficult than workin' their wheat fields. They started at the end closest to where Strouse had caught his last glimpse of Belle. It seemed the most logical area she might have wandered into, though John questioned if she would have done so in her newest and prettiest dress. A few years back she would have, but now she was beginning to see herself as a young woman. She had discarded the whims of a child.

"Here's the part, Tom, where yuh shouldn't be standin' on no ladder. Around 4:00 p.m. on this sultry Monday afternoon, the search committee found Mary. As Grandpa Strouse, John, Fred, and others combed the big woods, they heard Meister scream, 'Oh my God! Oh my God!' At first Meister thought a pig had stretched out in the mud, but it was Belle's pink dress. Her naked body lay beside it."

CHAPTER 11 — WORDLESS HORROR

A dark ridge of clouds fringed the sky like a shawl too sinister to wear.

"All the men was silent. The search committee's senses clogged. The sight of her defiled body, the obvious vile touchin', the sound of the pigs still chewin', contrasted with quiet gasps of the men. Nauseatin' smells clawed their way through the air. Somethin' metal-like coated their tongues. The effects of the cold full moon and the hot summer sun saturated the trampled ground. The men could see, hear, smell, and taste the massacre both them orbs had illuminated. Now they had no choice but to touch her remains.

"When they shooed the pigs away, it was obvious the torn and soiled pink dress hung only by the belt at her waist. They found her head close-by, partly eaten by the hogs.

"Not even the farmers could stand the thought of retrievin' her body parts. After getting' permission from a local doctor who examined her remains, one of them, no one would say who, bravely picked up her skull and lower jaw. The only clothin' left on her, other 'n the pink belt, was her shoes and socks. By this time, John, Grandpa Strouse, and Fred was there.

"Some wondered why the belt remained, but then saw it still looped onto the dress, which had been ripped off all the way down the front line of buttons, cinnamon pink fabric tatters still attached. They figured, if she'd gone down willingly, she'd have removed her foot coverings first, most every woman does, or so I've been told.

"One of the farmers carefully wrapped Mary's remains in a horse blanket. Yuh know, Tom, some was already gettin' ideas about who might have done it.

"John Sitterley carried her home, his tears spottin' the dust on the blanket. Fred hurried ahead to try to soften the blow fer Sarah.

"Fred found her standing at the door. 'Sarah.' Fred choked. 'We found Mary's body at the far end of the big woods. John's coming with her now.' Fred had tears of his own, most he'd ever cried when full-grown. He couldn't stop 'em though it wasn't the German-way for anyone ever to cry, 'specially not a man.

"Sarah was in shock. You can imagine, thinkin' Mary was safe at her grandfolks, then this. Sarah clutched a remnant of green bonnet ribbon. Maggie had sent extra gist in case one frayed or tore.

"Sarah couldn't speak. Fred ushered her to a chair. She wondered but didn't ask. Her eyes questioned Fred. He didn't answer. It were enough gist to process Mary was dead.

"Fred worried about leavin' Sarah alone, but the others wasn't far behind, so when they stepped on the property, he left. He needed to forewarn Kate and had one other task to perform.

"All he said to Kate was, 'We found Mary.' The rest was written on his face. Since Fred knew his wife would help clean the body, he thought to try to brace her fer the shock of what she was about to experience, so he added, 'We found her body in with Wienman's hogs. She'd most likely been there since yesterday.'

"Kate was well aware pigs would eat anything, even each other. An image of their pointed teeth registered in her brain. She tried to brace herself for what Fred hadn't told. Kate had helped prepare other bodies fer burial, but never a girl Belle's age who she loved like a daughter, whose condition was likely massacred.

"Kate's hands shook as she gathered flowers. She thought to take some powder and cornstarch. Kate's mother sent a beautiful silk scarf, a treasure belongin' to a grandmother who hadn't made the trip from the old country.

"Her mind numbed. It wasn't searchin' fer no song.

"Meanwhile, Fred grabbed a handful of square nails, and positioned 'em in his mouth. He lifted five fine oak boards they'd intended to use for a cabinet in Kate's kitchen. The cabinet would wait. John and Sarah's needs demanded their immediate attention.

"As Kate assembled the items in her basket, she heard hammerin' comin' from the barn. It was loud, fast, and furious, but no louder or faster or more furious than the poundin' of her heart."

CHAPTER 12 — THE LAST PETAL

A cloud eclipsed the sun. Beneath its blur, the sun resembled the moon. No rays were visible. No breeze stirred. Even the flies were unconventionally quiet.

Tom thought he noticed old Phil's eyes watering again. Attempting to clear his throat, Phil choked out his usual beginning, "Let me tell yuh about what we think occurred. We think when she came to the east-most corner of the woods, Belle probably stopped by the lilies.

"J. H. Day, in the little book he published shortly after her death, didn't mince words when he described the pigs or the perpetrators. Day said the animals was 'less ferocious than the human beasts.'

"At the jail, we could reconstruct quite a bit from the inquest. The bruises on her left arm indicated a hand must have grabbed her from behind because marks shaped like fingers circled the front of her arm. He come from behind. He used his left hand. She probably tried to scream before his right palm clamped tight over her mouth. She must have tasted his sweat and grime. His fingernails dug deep into her skin. She scraped her free arm as she elbowed, but the fightin' did no good. The attack tore a green ribbon from her bonnet. The search committee found her bonnet but not the missin' ribbon.

"She most likely wondered what he wanted. She had no money. She mighta thought to keep one, but she'd given both coins in the offerin'.

"As he dragged her into the woods, her pink dress caught on a thorny bramble. It ripped the skirt, leavin' it shredded.

"When the monster shoved her to the ground, he yanked at her bodice. He pulled so hard, he dislodged all the buttons, each with a pink fabric scrap still attached. The damage to the garment followed from her neck to the hem of her skirt.

"Wedgin' Mary's palms together, the beast clamped her fingertips in his mouth and bit down hard. His teeth marks remained. The trees lapped her screams onto a thousand leafy tongues and swallowed 'em whole. No one 'cept the woodland creatures and the villains heard.

"When they mounted her small body, she fought back with her shoes. Judgin' from their condition, she tried to kick and scrape, but mostly she dug grass and mud. Her small frame weren't no match fer their's.

"Once the rapes was over, we think one of them used her locks to lift her naked body, because a fist-full of her hair was found. From the looks of it, the thick smell of semen hung fer a long time in the sultry summer air.

"In an attempt to silence her, her skull was bashed with a section of fallen limb. Blood spurted onto the club and seeped through Belle's ringlets.

"I figure when they done the deeds, Mary musta thought she'd never be the first to bathe again."

CHAPTER 13 — PREPARATION FOR BURIAL

It's as difficult to give death as it is to give birth.

By now the big bubbles in Tom's bucket were gone, and only foam remained on the surface of the water. Old Phil sighed. "After this part, it should be safe fer yuh to git back on the ladder.

"Within a short time, the neighbor ladies congregated. The funeral would be Tuesday. Mary's already decomposin' corpse couldn't be kept any longer in the 'cessive heat. John had kept her covered with the blanket, but he couldn't cover the smell.

"No one wanted Sarah to see Mary's condition. Two of the women scurried her into the back bedroom to pick out burial clothes. Meanwhile, the others drew lots of water. They grabbed the lye soap from the kitchen. They wished the clock would stop tickin' so loud. The odor of the hogs, a day of death, and the lurk of evil enveloped the Sitterley's beautiful parlor. "One of the women whispered, 'Thank God some of her face is left.'

"They devised a plan. Each would have an area she cleaned and made presentable. When Fred arrived with the casket, they would lay Mary's cleaned torso in first, then position her head and jaw. They would wrap the pretty scarf from the old country 'round her neck and chin to hide the severed area. Even these farm women, some who'd single-handedly birthed and buried their own babies, was queasy.

"Fred helped John place the casket on a bench. The two christened it with tears. The rest of the search committee stood wordless on the Sitterley porch, starin' at their wheatfields.

The women used powders and perfumes to attempt to mask the smell. Gloves hid the marks on Mary's fingers where the the women noticed the bites was flat, not pointed. The ladies put pieces of tea-stained muslin over the places missin' muscle, skin, and bone, hopin' to create a less shockin' effect. Once her hair, face, and body was ready, they positioned lilies and other flowers around and over the damaged areas. It looked like she rested in a sweet bed of posies, sniffin' their scents, though the pigs had eaten part of her nose.

"Mary's least damaged side would be closest when the men pushed the bench against the parlor wall. They hoped any family viewin' her would not see her true condition in the darkened room. They 'specially worried about Sarah, Grandpa and Grandma Strouse, Marion, and her older brothers. John had already seen the worst. Fred would nail the casket shut before goin' home. No one at the funeral would view her body.

"Sarah chose the striped dress Mary wore for her tintype. Another of the women spoke, 'What would we have done had Mary not had two Sunday dresses?' The clock seemed to tick louder than ever. When the women finished, Mary floated in a floral sea. Fragrances overpowered most of the smell of death.

"Sarah was brought into the room. One of the women who had lost a child tried to encourage her, 'You'll get through this.'

"Sarah whispered, 'I don't want to.'

"At the casket, she reached out to touch 'Belle. Mary's skin was rock hard, her face, powdery white, the color of Sarah's lye soap. From the side view in the Sitterley's dimly lit parlor, she looked like Mary, but ghostly. John moved from his chair to stand with his wife. He knew more than he wanted to know and had seen more'n he had wanted to see.

"What the women had accomplished offered relief to John. It would leave him with a better memory than the sight in the woods. But even the gruelish Civil War hadn't prepared him. John wasn't the same. It would be years before he would happily joke and tease again. Sarah continued to clench the remnant of green ribbon.

"Before leavin', Kate worked on the bar of soap. She wanted it pure, like she'd found it. Usin' a knife, she shaved off specks of blood and dirt, skin and bark, grass and hair. Kate scrubbed hard to smooth the edges. She put the soap back in its dish, hopin' Sarah wouldn't think about what its last use had been. She threw the water out the back door. Kate heard thunder. Lightnin' filled the sky. Then all was still.

"Meanwhile, in the kitchen, the women disposed of the food Sarah had left fer Mary. I know it sounds strange, but they throwed it out to the pigs."

CHAPTER 14 — THE FUGITIVE

A red-tailed hawk flew with legs and feet hanging straight down, claws extended, ready to capture prey.

Tom climbed the ladder and grabbed the cleaning rag. The water felt cold, but he determined he'd use what he had.

"This part's about Henry's boys and the peddlers. Early on Monday before the community knew Mary'd come up missin', Jake and Abs walked the four or more miles back home from the state line while Mcleod and Andrew drove southwest to Jay City, Indiana. It would be their second stop fer rags on their return to Ft. Wayne where they worked fer A.J. Dillingham.

"Cousin Andy Jaxton, the one called 'The President,' told me later he was disappointed they weren't takin' the plank road runnin' through Shanesville and on to Ft. Wayne. Havin' grown up along it at Huntington, Indiana, and battlin' neuralgia, Andrew favored the smoother route, and couldn't understand Mcleod's logic or lack thereof. But Mcleod wasn't carin' anythin' about logic.

"Andy remembered thinkin', *Why did we have to leave so early? Why did we head south to go north? I'm sure we could have found rags on the smoother route.*

"All day on Monday, The President tried his best to reconstruct a growin' pile of events what left him frustrated and confused. He carefully assembled the stack in the exact order of how they'd occurred.

"The President considered it peculiar about both the ribbon and the booze for breakfast, but he thought the event with his horses the most unusual of all, since they normally stayed calm in every situation. He'd never had them try to run away, yet, they went stark ravin' mad out in the middle of nowhere fer no foreseeable reason.

"Andy recalled how when Jake and Ab left to walk home from the state line, both looked like they was gettin' sick. Perhaps it was his father's work as a doctor which made The President pay attention. Andy didn't recall his cousins havin' the ashen ague before they arrived at the woods. Andy couldn't stop thinkin': *The ribbon, the booze, the ague, and my horses going crazy all happened at the same spot.*

"After their second stop on Tama Road, Mcleod seemed to be in a hurry again. As the peddlers headed south, tin rattled with every turn of the wheel and bump in the road. As dust flew, Andy's sciatica kicked in, and he worried he might also develop a migraine.

"In Jay City, even before they relieved themselves, or bartered fer the rags, Mcleod paused to tie the crumpled green ribbon onto his horse's bridle. As he adjusted it, Andy saw a smirk slither from the head peddler's lips. *Obviously, Mcleod has no intention of including the ribbon with the rags. Why didn't he have Jake tie the ribbon on the bridle when they first found it if it's so important, and this was why he wanted it?*

"The President's suspicions grew tall. The sequence of events pelted his thoughts like a bad hail storm. He decided to try to pry some information from Mcleod. He knew how nasty Mcleod got when questioned, but it seemed safe to fish by commentin', 'I didn't like the looks of my cousins. They had a down appearance. Did you notice it, too?'

"Mcleod didn't even give Andy a sideways glance regardin' his question. He ignored Andy like Abs had ignored his question about the stop on Tama Road. Mcleod's lack of response conjured up more uneasy feelin's. Most people woulda rendered some kind of answer, either in agreement or disagreement, or 'I didn't notice...' or some theory of explanation, like '...maybe it was 'cause we hadn't eaten any breakfast.' Usually Mcleod would have snapped back with a snide remark implyin' Andy had asked another stupid question.

"Mcleod's mannerisms deposited more barnacles on the hull of The President's brain. It felt as tight as his migraines. It give Andy the feelin' his co-worker was hidin' somethin' big… somethin' way more than booze. As the peddlers turned north, Andy wondered what the three was avoidin'

"Andrew remembered a passin' remark from Abs about where the trio had gone on Sunday. Absalom had said, 'We was out findin' a girl.'

"Andy also recollected Mcleod asked Jake, 'Did you see any girls come this way?'

"Andy concluded, *Maybe the ribbon belongs to the girl they went to find? It's not a good sign it's torn and dirty!*

"He recalled his own reaction to Ab's words about 'finding a girl.' He'd said, 'You should never infringe on anyone's rights that way!' Somethin' in Ab's voice caused Andy to scold even though he didn't have all the details."

"After acquirin' rags in Jay City, the peddlers traveled without further conversation between wagons. As they neared Ft. Wayne, President Jaxton discovered yet another barnacle. On Tama Road, before they got to the state line, Abs confided, 'Mcleod wanted me to come along all the way back to the big city with you, but Pa said I should stay here.'

"Why in tarnation would he want Absalom, of all my cousins, to come with us? He certainly wouldn't draw any customers. For sure, he'd slow us down. Could it be Mcleod is afraid Absalom might tell more about 'finding a girl?' He's like a little kid who can't keep a secret for long. He wouldn't let it leak back home if he wasn't there.

"The President had a revelation: *Maybe Mcleod thought havin' Ab along would provide the opportunity to silence him forever!*

"The trip back allowed the head peddler to pick up on Andy's leeriness. Durin' the lengthy journey, the shyster musta done some rememberin' of his own.

"We figure all Henry's house slept 'cept the one who went back to take a last look. The moon exerted its fierce pull on his fence-post soul. His boots crunched through the forest debris. Slinkin' back, he found her body right where he'd left it, close to the brambles. She looked dead. The clubbin' rendered her unconscious, but she musta been breathin' shallow. If she recovered, she'd tell. Not enough had been done.

CHAPTER 15 — GRANDPA STROUSE'S TRIAL

Fireflies competed with the stars. Neither provided sufficient light.

Tom retrieved a much-needed bucket of fresh water. Bubbles mounded over the top and slopped onto the floor as the custodian climbed the ladder. Tom paused for a clean-up.

Phil said, "Bet you's glad you didn't spill everything. Let me tell yuh, whilst you dry the drops, how it was for Grandpa Strouse. Heaven had been punctured twice. His bucket was empty 'cept fer his tears.

"Strouse was well-respected in Liberty Township. Neighbors came to him to git information about 'most every farmin' dilemma. He was an icon on Tama Road. The loss of his daughter somehow elevated his position, and now, this.

"Strouse felt the full responsibility fer not protectin' Mary. Other'n the murderer or murderers, he was the last person to see her alive.

"Though everyone said, 'children should be seen and not heard,' Strouse wasn't able to apply this to his grandchildren. He tried to listen to 'em. Mary was the closest to his heart after the death of her mama.

"Strouse couldn't get rid of the thought of Belle bein' warned in her dream. He knew from Bible stories their great importance all through time and could list them from the Joseph with the coat to the Joseph in the stable. Night visions saved lives in both them stories. Even though he slept through Quaker meetings, Strouse remembered the second Joseph bein' cautioned to move to another land before Herod ordered the murder of all the little boys.

"Mary's experience appeared similar…the sacrifice of an innocent. Strouse sensed the angel in her dream musta been Susannah. But he'd made light of her dream by jokin' about raspberry pie. Grandpa Strouse felt if he wouldn't have slighted Belle's premonition, the crime would not have happened. He never did forgive himself.

"On the Monday night after they found her body, Strouse fell into a restless sleep, and had a devastatin' dream of his own.

"Grandpa Strouse saw himself, small in stature. A giant judge in a black robe sat behind an enormous bench. The judge questioned him, 'Strouse, did you or did you not do the unthinkable and ignore the warning in your granddaughter's dream?'

"Strouse answered feebly, 'I did, Your Honor.'

"The judge accused, 'You ignored a second warning! Did you or did you not see Alexander Mcleod and your neighbor boy, Absalom, leave church early?'

"Strouse's voice cracked: 'Yes, your honor.'

'And third, Mr. Strouse, did you or did you not allow your beautiful young granddaughter to walk down the road alone, paying little attention to your own uneasy feelings, and lazily soothing them by only watching her until she was out of sight rather than walking with her? Did you instead eat your dinner and take your afternoon nap?'

"The judge's voice was doin' a crescendo, and Strouse's was in a pianissimo as he answered, 'I did.'

'You were the last person other than the perpetrators to see her alive, were you not?'

"By now the judge's voice was so loud, Grandpa covered his ears. Any pride Strouse had ever felt was gone. His body was bent and stooped almost to the floor. Having no voice left, Strouse gist nodded.

'Grandpa Strouse, you are guilty as charged. You and you alone could have saved her! I sentence you on all counts. I sentence you to life…'

"Strouse was wringin' wet when he awoke. He didn't sleep the rest of the night. Somethin' had to be done. He felt personally liable. Ignorin' his responsibility would render him guilty on an additional count of neglect. As a leader in their church and in their community, and as Mary's beloved grandfather, it was up to him to help find who did this. A searin' suspicion lingered in his mind. It was pointed out in his dream: 'two had left the church early.' Even though he was a pacifist, this time Strouse could not 'turn the other cheek.'"

CHAPTER 16 — THE LAW

A forest of spider-web targets attached to blades of dew-laden grass. The webs were equal in width and height, and evenly distributed. All aligned at the same angle, glistening like a regiment of spun soldiers in the early morning light. Maybe the spiders had determined the webs' distribution, but the grass determined their direction as it sought energy from the sun.

Tom emptied the water tainted with the blackened soot of a long, hard winter. He replenished it and the soap and was climbing the ladder when Old Phil awakened as fresh as the suds.

"Like the rest involved, Sheriff Thornton remembered every detail about what he'd done the Monday Mary's body was found. Early in the day, he'd walked through the wet grass, smashin' dew-laden blades and spider webs. He'd aimed his gun. Feathers flew when he shot the chicken hawk out of a nearby tree. He was purdy sure it had killed one of their prize hens.

"The previous week his wife got upset when their children collected the eggs and used 'em for mud pies. With seven children, Thornton's family needed them eggs. It was an even greater disaster to lose the chicken. Thornton was grateful the hawk was dead.

"Our sheriff was a giant of a man, honest, and strong, and brave. He had lots of common sense. He also still farmed with his brother, Dan. Previously, he'd served as township assessor. 'Cause of his background with the community, he easily got elected sheriff. He hoped to work the law into his farmin' schedule as readily as he had assessin'. He hired several deputies, includin' Dan.

"Eighteen seventy-two was a season of tall crops and taller humidity. The size of our sheriff matched the times. Late on Monday, Thornton, like all local farmers, was tryin' his best to git his wheat harvested 'fore rain set in.

"Thornton, Dan, and Thornton's oldest sons was workin' the field when Deputy Bill Johnson from Hopewell Township rode in at breakneck speed with the look of total horror on his face. Thornton could tell Bill hadn't come fer the usual chit-chat about crops or weekend drunks.

"There was no chattin', gist a deposit of the brutal facts. 'A thirteen-year-old girl in Liberty Township turned up missin' since Sunday church. The family thought she'd spent Sunday night at her grandparents. The community formed a search party. Meizer found her naked body thrown in with some hogs in the big woods on Tama Road. It's obviously a rape and, most likely, a savage murder. You need to come! We've got way more than us deputies can handle."

CHAPTER 17 — TUESDAY, JUNE 25, 1872

The risin' sun hit its head on a grey cloud bank where upon the clouds swallowed it whole. A slight breeze flowed. A few sprinkles touched the thirsty earth.

Tom noticed a layer of grime on the molding above the only window in Phil's room. As he washed the dirt from the ceiling, he removed it as well. Then the custodian paused for Mary's funeral.

"Let me tell yuh how it was, Tom. Kate knew she and Fred would have to come up with an explanation for their children. Saying 'Mary died' would be hard. What if Phebe or Anton asked, 'How did she die?' Kate decided to say, 'Mary's body got hurt and didn't work anymore. It couldn't keep her energy, so her energy left and went right to heaven.'

"Phebe cried. 'I don't want Mary's energy to be gone.'

"Kate said, 'It's not gone, Phebe. It's just not in her body anymore. Our bodies are like sacks or hot air balloons for our energy. Maybe Mary's flew right to heaven because I bet it's fast, huh, Anton?' Anton nodded and smiled a little at the thought.

"Surprisin'ly, neither asked how Mary got hurt. Maybe they gist knew their mama couldn't speak of it any more.

"They interred Mary's remains in the Chapel Cemetery. The cemetery is small and grassy, all clear of trees. It sets opposite the church. A big crowd gathered. People didn't work when neighbors needed comfortin'. All of Henry's family attended the funeral.

"The usual scriptures was read. The preacher spoke the part about, 'Yea though I walk through the valley of the shadow of death, I will fear no evil…' But how the heck do yuh not fear evil, Tom? It sure takes a lotta faith.

"Sarah told later how she had no prayers. She thought again, *You don't thank God for evil. I try to thank Him for everything like the Bible says, but how can I ever thank Him for this?*

"People saw Sarah standin' there in her black dress, tightenin' her grasp on the green ribbon. She rubbed it nervous-like 'tween her fingers, gently stroking the ribs.

"She said she remembered the trip to Maggie's store to purchase it. Her thoughts jumped around. She thought about when they got Mary's tin-type taken in her striped dress…the one she was now bein' buried in. She recalled happy times from their past three years together.

"Lookin' at the preacher's long beard brought the recollection of a story Mary told about her early childhood when she was about five, or six. Mary had been swingin' on the clothesline at Grandpa Strouse's. She knew the preacher would be comin', 'cause he came every Sunday fer dinner after his wife died, but still she continued swingin'.

"The minister thought he could duck under the line rather than walk the long way around. As Mary swung back, the rope caught his long-speckled beard, tanglin' in the course hairs, pulling hard. The preacher screamed. He even used a four-letter word.

"Mary joked how she was sure she was 'in line' for big trouble, but all the reverend said at dinner was 'Please pass the potatoes.'

"Mary confided her relief. Sarah could still see the look on Belle's face. Sarah's lips turned up ever so slightly over the funny memory.

"Kate sang at the burial, midst her own tears. A strong belief existed about singin' souls to heaven. Sarah said Kate's beautiful song made her think of the little bird on Mary's locket, in flight now, free from this world.

"One of the prayers was the Lord's prayer, which everyone said together. No one could ignore how 'Deliver us from evil' had new meanin' now. Sarah wondered if humans would ever escape evil, since, like Mary had said, 'evil' is 'live' spelled backwards. Sarah thought, *Evil is the distorted mirror image of what this life should and could be.*

"Standin' at the cemetery, Sarah glanced at Susannah's grave. At this moment, the strongest part of her emotional toolbox begun to surface. She thought a thought, which like a mighty wrench turned her ever so slightly in a new direction. She thought, *Mary's with her real mama now.* It was Sarah's first knowledge of somethin' other than yesterday's shrivelin' shock, and the pain punnishin' her soul.

"Sarah told how she tried to use her by-words to scrape away some of the darkness by saying, 'I'm so glad Mary is with Susannah,' but them words gist wouldn't come.

"She did manage this. She dropped the green ribbon on Susannah's grave. The piece bore little resemblance to what she'd clutched the previous day, 'cause now it was embroidered with her tears. Lettin' go allowed Sarah to think, *I can say thank you that Susannah was there to welcome Mary. They're both angels now.*

"Fred and several other men lowered the casket. John, Grandpa Strouse, Mary's two older brothers and her twin,

Marion, took turns shovelin' in the first dirt. Crumble by crumble and clod by clod, heavy clay covered the walnut trim.

"Sarah looked away as the preacher said his final lines, 'Ashes to ashes and dust to dust.'

"Much later Sarah told Kate how standin' in the graveyard she began reasonin', 'The earth's our real mother. We come from her and to her we return. We are like the earth walking, since her food and water make us. Mary has gone back to be with both of her real mothers.'

"Leanin' on John's arm, Sarah sobbed quietly. John loaded her into their buggy. They rode west. John snapped the lines, drivin' past the big woods as fast as the ruts would allow. Neither of the Sitterleys looked at the spot."

CHAPTER 18—WEDNESDAY, JUNE 26, 1872

It took a full hour for morning to birth the sun.

Having finished the ceiling, Tom began the walls. Tom thought, *Phil's story is becoming worse as his room becomes better.*

"Back in Ft. Wayne, Andy and Mcleod was unloadin' freight, organizin' it, and reloadin' their wagons fer the next week's outing. The temperature and humidity hadn't changed. The three rivers runnin' through the big city spouted a stiflin' sauna. As the two stacked crates, they pulled their handkerchiefs to wipe sweat from their brows. Andrew noticed Mcleod's. It was speckled with dots.

"The peddlers worked at 172 Calhoun Street, a main thoroughfare, located close to the Toledo, Wabash, and Western Railway Freight Depot, which sits between Calhoun and Harrison. The heat from the steam engines made conditions more unbearable. By the week's end, Mcleod reeked.

"Others questioned Andy, 'What's with him? He stinks way worse than the rest of us. Mcleod smells like a darn polecat.'

"President Jaxton said, 'Maybe it's because he wore two shirts from Sunday through Wednesday. 'Had to be more'n his head that's been hot.'

"Andy told me later, 'On Wednesday, when the temperature reached near a hundred, Mcleod decided to remove the striped shirt. I found myself glaring at the stains on the solid colored one. Mcleod saw me and reacted defensive-like. As if accusing me of being stupid, he said, "What are you looking at me for? I had a nose-bleed!"

"That skunk always tried to spray others first, hopin' they'd carry the stench and not notice it come from him."

CHAPTER 19 — THE EXUMATION

The surge between law and grace is perennial.

"On Wednesday, back at the cemetery, probably around the same time Mcleod took off his blood-stained shirt, Thornton met five doctors. From the upstairs bedroom, George could see a line of carriages parked alongside the tombstones. The men had shovels. George saw 'em unearth Mary's casket from under a mound of dirt and flowers. They covered their noses and mouths with kerchiefs. When they removed the lid from Belle's coffin, George checked the time. It was noon.

"This was done 'cause Thornton knew if he was to build a verifiable case, he'd need an official autopsy. The testimony of a few farmers and one local doctor, who only saw the body fer a short time in the shade of the woods, most likely wouldn't stand up in court. Before orderin' the autopsy, he got both

Strouse's and the Sitterley's permission. Thornton wasn't about to leave either 't' in his name uncrossed.

"As sheriff, this was one of Thornton's best decisions regardin' this case. As a father, it was his worst. Mary's small body and its condition branded Thornton's mind with its image and odor. Every time he'd see her remains in his memory, he'd git a tear. Her tortured state made him determined to find the demon who'd ravaged this young girl.

"It'll help you to understand our sheriff, Tom, if yuh know he and Jane had five sons in a row. Then, only two years before this all happened, Jane gave birth to their first little girl. Gist a year later, she had their second.

"Thornton was a softie 'round his little daughters with their bright eyes and delicate hair. He could only imagine how he would feel if this had happened to either of them. The emotions he embalmed at Mary's casket never did leave him.

"When completed, the doctors verified the rape. Most important, they confirmed a sharp object had been used to sever her head. Her throat muscles and ligaments wasn't torn, they was cut. Them edges was straight, not jagged or shredded. Mary hadn't been decapitated by somethin' that oinked.

"Thornton issued a five-hundred-dollar reward. It was the biggest ever in our area. Those funds coulda bought a lot of land back then.

"Since they was in the locality, the sheriff, Dan, and both Bills devoted every hour after the autopsy to questionin' the local residents, narrowin' the suspect list, and spreadin' the word about the five-hundred-dollar reward.

"At first, Thornton suspected all the men and grown boys, even John Sitterley, Mary's brothers, Grandpa Strouse, and Fred.

"It upset the community to be thought of as murderers, but everyone wanted the truth. Already in a state of fright over the prospect a two-legged predator or predators roamed their area, no girls was allowed to walk anywhere alone. Children old enough to understand slept on wood and dirt floors by their parents' beds, 'cause of how scared they was.

"Guns sat loaded and propped close to front doors in most every home. Durin' the day, Fred mounted his above the door frame. At night, he put it close at hand under his side of the bed. He slept with his arm hangin' down so's he could grab it quick. Fred had only ever used it to kill varmints. Though he would do so when needed, he didn't much like killin' for food, 'specially rabbits and pheasants. Their fur and feathers was so beautiful. He hated seein' 'em coated with blood. He gist couldn't stand to see anythin' suffer. If he had to kill for food, he wanted the shot to be sure. He'd put the animal out of its misery as fast as possible."

"It was easy fer Thornton to piece together when the murder happened. Mary was nearly home when she was attacked. Strouse told the approximate time they'd parted ways. Bein' familiar with her pattern, the Sitterleys knew when she would normally arrive at their house, even if she stopped to twirl some lilies.

"The residents on Tama generally could remember who went by since little traffic moved down the rutted road. Every unusual sound broke the stillness. Dogs barked. If someone passed, people would ask, 'I wonder who that was?' They'd quit work to look-see. The only labor done on Sundays related to feedin' themselves and their animals, so there was plenty of time fer nose-trouble. They knew each other's horses and buggies. They knew each other. No one reported seein' or hearin' anyone travelin' by after they arrived home from church on Sunday, June 23, 1872. No hoof prints or horse droppin's was found in the woods, so the person or persons had to have arrived on foot, but not on Tama Road—somebody woulda spotted 'em.

"Mary was the only one known to walk as far as the big woods from Liberty Chapel. Whoever did this musta been hiddin' in the woods, waitin'.

CHAPTER 20 — FRIDAY, JUNE 28, 1872

The night sky sparkled with a rare and brilliant clarity.
Occasionally, a great horned owl hooted. As tiny creatures
scurried through the grass below, the amazing bird moved its
yellow eyes and raised its enormous wings. It dropped its legs
and extended its claws.

The hands of the clock and Tom's stomach both pointed to noon. The custodian brought his lunch. An attendant delivered Phil's tray, but Phil didn't seem interested. Taking occasional bites, Phil talked between nibbles. Tom hoped the old man wouldn't choke since he tended to speak with his mouth full.

"Only five days after the murder, Thornton prepared to make five arrests. Unfortunately, two of 'em wasn't gonna be any cake walk.

"Ft. Wayne housed around eighteen thousand folks and was some fifty miles away. Thornton planned on takin' three deputies: Dan, Bill Johnson, and Bill Moore. He left me in charge of the jail."

Tom was the one who choked on his food. It had never occurred to him Phil might have been an officer of the law. If the old guy had said so, Tom had missed it. However, the custodian did remember Phil speaking like he'd been present when the murder was first discussed.

Phil scolded Tom, "Better chew it up, boy! It don't ever work to take big chunks, or try to swallow whole. 'Gotta' take things piece by piece."

"Thornton said before they left: 'At about ten or eleven miles per hour, with a stop in Decatur, I'm guessing this trip will take five or six hours one way. We'll have to refresh our horses. It'll be about twelve hours on the road if we don't have any glitches. If we find the suspects, we'll not take the risk of lodging them overnight.' Thornton realized expectin' 'em to actually be in Ft. Wayne was a big gamble. Fer all he knew, Mcleod mighta decided to bamboozle it back tuh Canada, or be out peddlin' or committin' yit another murder.

"I remember how Thornton paused before speakin', makin' sure he had everyone's full attention. He made direct eye contact with each deputy before he cautioned, 'Men, if we don't use our heads, we'll have to use our hands and feet. When we catch them, and catch them we will, we're not going to tell the prisoners why they're being arrested. I'm banking on them telling us. If we've got the right people, the truth will come out one syllable at a time. It's a trick I've used with my kids. All parents and teachers seem to know it. Tell them nothing, and eventually, someone will let something slip. It might come in small bits and take reassembling, like last week at my place with the eggs and mudpies. Our work here will be to put Humpty Dumpty back together again. The more egg shells they hand us, the less we'll have to find for ourselves. They'll have lots of opportunities on the return trip. Right before we lock them in their cells, we'll tell them'."

"Thornton's posse left around four a.m. They took the plank road from Shanesville. It dumped rain near Decatur. Mud gushed between the timbers as the horses' clunked along. Thornton was mighty glad fer the planks. Being stuck in the mud woulda made fer a giant glitch in the hitch.

"Our posse arrived in the big city a little after ten. Ft. Wayne bustled and hummed, bein' at the time the world's largest supplier of axles and wheels for the railroads. A place called Kunkle Valve had patented the safety valves fer steam engines—the business still operates, fer as I know. The city was modern in ways the sheriff and his deputies had never seen, like horse-drawn streetcars. Thornton said a surplus of road apples smelled way too ripe in the summer sun.

"Thornton was relieved, because he had no trouble locatin' the two peddlers, but he did have an adventure capturin' Mcleod. The varmint tried to escape. Fer Thornton, Mcleod's run marked his first admission of guilt.

"The peddler yelled to his co-workers, 'Help me!' But no one did. Good the boy was wearin' suspenders or he mighta lost his pants.

"Thornton alerted Dan, 'He's headed to the alley. Cut him off before he hops a train!'

"With the aid of his deputies, Thornton nabbed Mcleod before he got very far. Even then, the sprawly critter didn't come willin'ly. Dan and Thornton had to drag him back on his heels.

"'Mcleod ranted and raved, 'I didn't do nothing.'

"Thornton remarked, 'Then why are you running from something?'

"They struggled to load him. Finally, Thornton resorted to shovin' his pistol into the unprotected spot where the peddler's spinal cord slithered into his brain, sayin' 'Get your sorry butt in the wagon, Mcleod.'

"It was by far the most challengin' arrest of Thornton's first year bein' sheriff. He had a flashback to when his children ran to hide in the barn to escape punishment fer the egg/mud-pie escapade. It had taken the crack of a buggy whip to git his young-uns out from under their carriage.

"Thornton confiscated more than a tin peddler. One of our deputies located the missin' piece of green ribbon. When Thornton saw it tied on the peddler's bridle, he was sure it was an exact match to the one on Mary's bonnet.

"They also arrested Henry's nephew, Andrew Jaxton. Unlike Mcleod, The President didn't run. However, he did act perplexed, as though he was tryin' to solve somethin' himself. No evidence was found on him, or 'midst any of his possessions.

"Thankful for the food Annabelle had packed, Thornton and the deputies had no trouble eatin' lunch in front of the two they nabbed. Needin' time fer farmin', Thornton devoted the remainder of the return trip to procurin' information. He knew he couldn't afford to waste six hours. While Andy kept doin' what was asked, Mcleod showed himself to be a different part of a horse's body. The red-haired peddler remained uneasy and uncooperative. He lacked the calm of someone who had nothin' to hide.

"As they exited Ft. Wayne, Thornton noticed the head peddler place one boot on top of the other in an unnatural position. When Mcleod relaxed a bit further down the road, his foot slid onto the floor of the wagon revealin' a boot stained with what looked to be dry blood.

"Mcleod had turned up the cuffs on his shirt sleeves to try to hide similar stains. The blotches on his pants looked like he tried to wash 'em away. Mcleod had been a lot more successful cleanin' his pants than his shirt. Guess the peddler figured no one would try to find him in Ft. Wayne. He didn't know our sheriff had seen Mary's corpse.

"The attempts at disguise, even more than the blood itself, made Thornton certain he had his man. Thornton hollered back to Bill, 'You know, sometimes my kids steal cookies from the jar. When Jane catches 'em, they hold the cookies behind their backs to hide the evidence. It's interesting how this is coming to mind now'."

"Still Mcleod said nothin'. Thornton asked him point blank, 'Where were you last Sunday, June 23rd?'"

"He saw Mcleod quiver and avoid eye contact. The Sheriff wondered, *Is he takin' this intermission to try to remember? More likely, he's working on what kind of story to tell.*

"Lookin' away, Alexander Mcleod ignored Thornton's question in the same way he tried to evade bein' captured, and gist like he had avoided Andy's question about the ague. Our sheriff had seen the same kind of responses in people who thought about lyin' when he did the assessin', but most of the locals was basically honest and the truth 'ventually got told.

"Thornton leaned over to plant another seed 'midst the rusty hairs growin' out of Mcleod's thick skull. Our sheriff called the peddler's bluff with this comment: 'Silence can speak louder than words, Mcleod, just like actions can'."

"No major stops had been planned other than one. About twenty miles south of Ft. Wayne, Thornton saw a sign sayin', 'Decatur, Indiana. Population seventeen hundred.' Though more'n ten times smaller'n Ft. Wayne, Decatur also sported a lot of activity. They'd have to return to Washburn's Livery Stable to claim their horses. Thornton wisely decided to travel a couple of extra miles out of the way, because he knew the people in town might talk, 'specially those at the livery who'd already asked questions durin' their stop on the way. If someone said, 'So these are the boys you think mighta killed the girl,' Thornton would lose his edge of secrecy.

"Since Belle's body hadn't been found when the peddlers left on Monday morning, it weren't likely the prisoners would know anything about the crime unless they was involved.

"Outsmartin' human nature was a big part of Thornton's job.

"The sheriff remarked, 'An ounce of prevention's always worth at least a pound of cure.'

"So, Deputy Johnson walked the livery horses back into town all by himself. Thornton and the other Bill and Dan stayed with the prisoners—two with Mcleod, one with Andrew.

"Havin' switched steeds, they was a little south of Decatur when Alexander Mcleod finally decided he would answer Thornton's where-abouts question. So's you don't have to scratch yer head fer it and git suds in your hair, Tom, the sheriff's question was 'Where were you last Sunday, June the twenty-third?'

Phil picked up an old diary from his bedside table. He began reading what he'd written some fifty years prior, using a deeper tone to differentiate the sheriff from Mcleod:

'I was with Andy the whole time.'

'And where were you two during that time?'

'I went to church.'

'With Andy?'

'Andy didn't go to church'."

Tom jerked enough to jiggle the ladder and spill more suds.

After the peddler had contradicted himself several times, the sheriff pondered his options. It was then Thornton come up with the idea of stoppin' at the scene of the crime.

"As they got closer, Deputy Bill devised a plan of his own. He come up from the rear of the wagon and said, 'Andy just told us everything.'

"Mcleod exclaimed, 'My God, it can't be possible Andy has gone back on me!'

"As they neared the woods, Alex Mcleod seemed to be in a state of fear mixed with nervous anger. When the wagon rolled to within sight, this tellin' bit of truth popped right out of the peddler's mouth. 'I didn't hurt the gal.'

"The deputies had kept themselves quiet gist like Thornton had cautioned. No one had mentioned 'a girl' was 'hurt.' Mcleod's comment stirred Thornton's memory of his kids sayin', 'We don't know how eggshells got in the mud,' before anythin' was ever said about eggs or mud.

"By now the sky was as dappled as the peddler's words. When they came to a full stop by the big woods, Mcleod stared at the spot where the search committee found the bloody club. He could have looked at a million other places, yuh know. Thornton recognized how sometimes behavior gist plain shouts the truth.

"Thornton received little trainin' when he took office, however, our former sheriff did inject one interestin' insight. He told Thornton, 'People will oft show you the truth in one of two ways, they'll either laugh or cry.'

"Sure enough, the next emotion comin' from Mcleod was tears...no sobbin', gist a few drops. He couldn't stop the instant flow down those ruddy cheeks. Thornton pushed further. 'We know all about it Mcleod. You'd better fess up.'

"Mcleod looked away and said, 'I never committed adultery here or anythin' else. I never saw this bloody spot before.'

"As Mcleod spoke, his body showed more than his words. The peddler turned his eyes, his head, and his torso away, tellin' in triplicate he'd lied. He faced away from the truth.

"Thornton and me never did figure out his comment regardin' 'adultery.' We wondered if Mcleod was, in fact, married. Or did the tinner say it, 'cause he knew the girl wasn't married, and if she was single, by Biblical standards, rape wasn't adultry? Either way, it sure implied he knew somethin' about the murder, and knew darn well someone had fornicated in the woods.

"Based on Mcleod's other slips of the tongue, I believe the peddler didn't think through his answer. I think he was married. Though, other'n this comment, he never mentioned havin' a wife, let alone one named Mary."

"What they heard satisfied Thornton. Though late on an already long day, our sheriff headed around the corner to arrest the remainin' suspects.

"Seeing they were headin' to Henry's, Mcleod tried a tactic of his own: 'I need to talk with Henry.' After rethinkin' his boldness, Mcleod rephrased it kinda polite, 'Please, let me talk to Henry. It's important.'

"Thornton wondered, *Is the peddler trying to construct an alibi, or is he crafting a plan to escape?* The sheriff had begun to unlock Mcleod's mind, and them was the only two keys seemin' to fit. The 'please' approach angered Thornton when his children tried it. The sheriff saw it as a sign of desperation.

"Thornton approached Henry, 'I'm looking for three of your sons.'

'Boys ain't home. Figure they're about half mile down the road.'

"Thornton said to Dan, 'What's another half mile when we've covered nearly a century's worth?'

"Mcleod tried again. 'Well, if you won't let me talk to Henry, at least let me talk with his boys.' 'Please...'

"For Thornton, givin' Mcleod the chance woulda been like givin' his own sons time to manufacture a story about the eggs. If they each regurgitated the same tall tale, it might seem true. Thornton told Dan, 'I'm thirty-six years old. I wasn't born yesterday.'

"It was on the half-mile trek to arrest the last three suspects, when Thornton opted to shoot from the hip. He squeezed the trigger quickly hopin' Mcleod would respond the same way in kind of a verbal dual. If our sheriff said it just right, maybe the peddler wouldn't even take a fraction of a second to think before firin' back.

"It worked. Thornton had Dan record Mcleod's exact words fer evidence.' He'd had Dan do the same with the other incriminatory comments.

Tom saw Phil sit up a little straighter as he readied himself. The old man pushed his glasses back up on his nose to read.

'Who was with you out in the woods about two o'clock on Sunday?'

'Ja-Jake, Abs.'

"Thornton couldn't help noticin' all the implications in the peddler's answer.

Jake and Abs, but not George or Andy. The President also had cast nothin' George's way or his own, makin' the first match in what was bein' said.

"All of Mcleod's malfunctions fit perfectly…'girl, bloody spot, adultry, Jake-Abs' with *him* in the woods.

"Andy and Mcleod hadn't been allowed to converse, and Thornton knew Andy couldn't hear from the back of the wagon. However, the sheriff was too focused to risk an error by prematurely exoneratin' President Jaxton, or by not arrestin' George. Neither had airtight alibis. He said to the deputies, 'A bird in hand is worth three in the bush, and in our case, five jail birds are worth at least fifteen. I'd rather chance being wrong than to have anyone guilty escape.'

When he finally collected Henry's three sons, our sheriff found 'em completely different. The oldest was short, blond, and unkept, whilest the middle stood tall, dark-haired, and handsome. The youngest looked wide-eyed and nervous. The only similarity between them boys was not one of 'em fought the arrest.

"Thornton and his crew packed the two peddlers and Henry's three youngsters into the wagon, separatin' them as much as possible. Thornton admitted, 'We've got ourselves a handful'."

CHAPTER 21 – DUCK LEGS

Everything is a flower sometime.

"I can remember clearly when they arrived at the jail. This part I know firsthand. Guess I haven't filled yuh in much on my life or my job.

"When I was young, I got a nickname. People called me 'Duck Legs.' They said, 'I walked like a duck and moved my arms the same way'."

Tom slipped slightly on the soapy rung. Grateful he hadn't laughed, the custodian continued working like Phil had said nothing humorous.

"Havin' been teased a lot, I felt proud when Thornton asked me to be one of his deputies and handed me a badge. Thornton called me 'Deputy D.L.' or 'Phil' and most never called me 'Duck Legs.'

"Since the sheriff and the other deps didn't live in town, I manned the jail overnight and on the weekends. Thornton wanted a full-time resident who didn't occupy a cell. In exchange fer handin' out the bread and water, I got free room and board and my meals delivered by Annabelle, who lived gist down the street. Fer me, her food cinched the deal. There was a decent salary, too. Thornton knew I was dependable.

"Our county averaged only a few major incidents a month. Back then, most men farmed. They was too exhausted when they finished their work to be criminals. We dealt a lot with the inebriated, saw some sporadic thievin', vandalism, and a little counterfeitin'. The county had no sanitarium, so in addition to bein' the drunk tank, we provided space fer the insane. I've heard some of the deranged is now bein' kept here."

Phil hoped his custodian would comment concerning whether the Infirmary housed those with mental problems so he'd know for sure, but Tom was restricted regarding what he should and shouldn't say about residents. Having gotten no reply, D.L. figured Tom's lack of a response resembled Alexander Mcleod's. Deputy D.L. had his answer...

"The only downside, back then, of dealin' with my job was one of the crazies made me a target fer dodge ball and used his fecal matters fer the ball. Other 'n those moments, I loved my life and my job, that is, until I got the murder suspects to guard.

"It was the middle of the night, somewhere on the swing 'tween Friday and Saturday, when I opened the door fer Thornton, the three deps, and five new prisoners. Thornton entered one on one with Mcleod, pistol in hand. Every cell in our jail was sweatin' more than us humans. I hoped with all the 'cessive heat and moisture, our walls wouldn't melt and set our new brood free.

"When I first heard about Mary, I didn't know the meanin' of the word 'decapitated,' but I didn't want to show my ignorance by askin'. 'Ventually, when I learned the murderer had cut off her head. I 'member sayin', 'This wasn't gist the killin' of a defenseless young girl. This was out 'n out savagery.' I wasn't so sure about havin' these kind under my watch, not knowin' who they might try butcherin' next and all."

CHAPTER 22 — SATURDAY, JUNE 29, 1872

The heart-shaped leaves of the redbuds shivered ever so slightly in morning's early glow. The sun jolted their sap in an effort to restore greenness. Birds chirped sweet songs. The scent of honeysuckle permeated the morning mist. Petals dropped.

"The events on Tama Road etched everyone with a different pattern, but with no less deep cuts. Some nursed head-guilt along with heart-sorrow. Sarah regretted buyin' Mary the pretty pink dress. John and Grandpa Strouse regretted makin' light of Belle's dream. Fred regretted not investigatin' the flock of birds Anton had spotted swarming from the big woods.

"Broken in spirit and fightin' the images of Mary's tortured body, the only singin' Kate had left was her children's lullabies. She found it impossible to leave Phebe, Anton, and Emma alone. Getting' up to check on 'em was robbin' her of much-needed sleep.

"Both Fred and Kate experienced nightmares. Kate said in hers she saw Mary's tortured body and she scrubbed the same bloody bar of soap over 'nd over again. No matter how hard she tried, she couldn't git it clean.

"In Fred's, he made tiny caskets and put 'em in long rows. All of them of oak with walnut trim. Like Kate, he could not finish. There was always one more child-size burial box to construct.

"They struggled to keep up with work. Fred's corn grew 'knee-high before the Fourth of July,' but so did the weeds. In a normal summer, Fred woulda spent an hour or so eliminatin' weeds when the sun was barely risin', the air was cooler, and too much moisture existed to harvest grain. He'd be wet from dew before he got soaked with sweat. He'd be nervous if a weed bloomed, 'cause fer sure he didn't want it goin' to seed.

"But in only one week's time, an army of green invaders blossomed over his corn. Fred had spent the early hours helpin' John whose desire to work was depleted.

"Meanwhile, Kate's cookin' turned into a sorry monitor of the mood swellin' within her. Anguish rose, but the bread didn't. Kate forgot to add the yeast. When she remembered, she overheated the milk, and scalded the very life out of the dough. She hurriedly threw food together. It was the first their cabin smelled of burnt offerin's.

"On Saturday mornin', Phebe had had enough. She broke through Kate's demise by questionin' the wordin' of her daddy's mealtime prayer. In her little voice and with the utmost sincerity, she asked her mama, 'If it's 'by God's hands we all are fed,' why does our food 'taste-us' so bad this week'?"

"Stunned, Kate looked at Phebe as tears ran down her own cheeks and seeped into the pancake batter. Touchin' Phebe's little arm, and eye to eye with her, Kate said, 'It's not God's fault, Phebe. God is giving us this food from the plants and animals just fine, but Mama is having trouble preparing it'."

"Phebe's early attempts at human logic was understandable. Some of the adults blamed their Creator, too, fer the bad batch of batter they'd been served.

"Kate said. 'It's like this, Phebe, sometimes things are just better than other times, includin' Mama's cooking of God's food. You know how sometimes the sun shines so pretty and sometimes it goes behind a cloud, or goes night-night'?"

Phebe nodded.

"Kate continued, 'You remember the rainbow we saw last week? When it storms, its pretty colors show sunshine is returning. Mama will make you a pancake shaped like a rainbow for your breakfast. It'll remind us of the coming back of the good life, including Mama's cooking of God's food."

"Phebe smiled her pretty little smile. Kate made five rainbow pancakes without burning them. She also made the usual round ones. Kate told Phebe, 'The round ones are the sun.'

"Phebe slipped a pancake sun over top of a pancake rainbow. Her mama spread it with golden butter and drizzled it with thick maple syrup.

"After Fred's prayer, Kate ate rainbow and sun griddle cakes and considered what she'd fix next fer her family. She determined she'd take somethin' fresh to the Sitterleys and a hug fer Sarah, who still spent most of her time sittin' at the kitchen table, starin' at the message she'd writ on Mary's slate.

"By reachin' out to Sarah, Kate halted the focus on her own pain. It was up to her to keep life goin' fer their family. The best she had to give come from her kitchen."

"By Saturday afternoon, the word of Friday's arrests had spread throughout the community. Some said they caught 'em in Ft. Wayne, others said in Dayton. Fred and Kate heard two of the five was the tin peddlers. They was shocked to hear the other three was their neighbor boys."

"Kate commented to Fred, 'Maybe the persnickety peddler would be glad for a molasses cookie today.'

"The grapevine, who'd told the arrests was in Dayton, also said there'd be a court hearin'. Fred learned a hearin' is sort of a 'trial before the trial' to be sure enough evidence exists to invest the time and money in a trial.

"The neighbor said, 'Hearings only last about a half an hour to two hours at the most.'

"Fred and Kate decided they would attend to support John and Sarah and Mary's memory, though doin' a lot of John's work, as well as his own, left Fred no minutes to spare, 'specially with the year's plentiful harvests of wheat, straw, and hay. Fred and Kate was also aware they might get called to the witness stand. Perhaps Fred would have to tell about Anton's sighting of the birds and approximate the time he spotted them fly out of the big woods.

"Meanwhile, the neighborhood men had joined forces to finish John's wheat before resumin' their own harvests. The women established a schedule fer deliverin' food to the field and to the Sitterley's, even though John and Sarah was hardly eatin' anythin'. The whole community would sacrifice additional time to attend the hearin'. Countin' the search for Mary's body, and her funeral, and the hours donated to help provide the food, and farm for the Sitterleys, the residents of Tama Road had already lost about a week during the busiest farmin' season of summer.

"Everyone figured Grandpa Strouse, and John, and Sarah would all have to testify, and wondered how they'd be able. The women who'd help hide Belle's horrific condition knew Sarah would hear a full disclosure of what happened and Mary's state when they found her body. John knew this, too, so he tried his best to soften the blow: 'You know about hogs, Sarah. What happened to our Mary was worse than hogs.' "

CHAPTER 23 — ANDY

In summer's soil, weed and flower fight their battles side by side.

As Tom climbed back down to reposition his ladder, Deputy D.L. initiated a new train of thought. He switched his focus back to the jail.

"It was the mornin' after the arrests when we got our first squeal. It come from Andrew Jaxton. What Andy told, and the way he told it made a lot of sense to us because the truth is always in the timeline. Andy had the timeline down-pat.

"While waitin' his turn to be questioned, the sequence of those events stuck like a row of aged barnacles to Cousin Andy's mind. Each happenin' notched precisely perfect with the precedin' one as he put 'em in the order. of how they'd happened. He told me his reconstructions went somethin' like this…

'Only Mcleod and Ab come home from church early, but then Mcleod and Ab left with Jake right after Jake arrived—no waiting for dinner.

'Before leavin', the huckster asked Jake, 'Did you see any girls headed this way after church?'

'When they returned, Ab told quite clearly, "We was out finding a girl…'

"When Sheriff Thornton verified they'd been arrested for the murder of *a girl*, Andrew said, 'I'm ready to give my statement'."

"It upset The President when the sheriff pushed him to include George's name. Andy was pretty sure George was home all day on Sunday, but Thornton said it was a necessary precaution since Andy was not with George one hundred percent of the time, and since unbeknownst to him, George might have decided to follow the rest of 'em after he and Uncle Henry climbed the stairs."

"The President did respect his namesake in terms of right and wrong, and calling a spade a spade. I kept the affidavit Andy signed—prob-ly weren't supposed to, but as I was the one who penned the copies fer Thornton, I gist made one extra."

Deputy D. L. opened an old tin box to retrieve the document. As he did so, he accidentally slid his scratched spectacles off the end table and onto the floor.

Tom halted his work to retrieve them. He was glad to see they hadn't broken.

Phil said, "Thanks, Tom. I'll be needin' these fer this readin'."

Once he'd adjusted his eyewear to avoid interference from a line on the left lens, Phil began:

"Before me, one of the Justices of the Peace for said county, personally came Andrew Jaxton, who being duly sworn according to law, deposeth and saith that verily he believes, that Alexander McLeod, Absalom. ., Jacob. ., and George. . . on the 23rd day of June, in the year of our Lord one thousand eight hundred and seventy-two, in the county of. . .aforesaid, in the attempt to perpetrate a rape upon Mary Arabelle. . .and while so attempting to perpetrate said rape did then and there purposely, unlawfully and feloniously kill and murder the said Mary. . . And further this deponent saith not."

"ANDREW JAXTON"

"Sworn to and subscribed before me at the county aforesaid, this 29th day of June, A.D. 1872."

"In his original deposition, Andrew had gist said "rape a girl" since he didn't know her name. The justice of the peace added Mary's name."

Duck Legs said, "Guess you've noticed, Tom, how I leave out some surnames. I do this 'cause relatives still lives 'round here, and you might happen to know 'em...I don't want to cause 'em any harm.

"Andrew told me he'd come to a conclusion about why his horses was so agitated. He said, 'I'm sure they could smell her blood.'

"Yuh know, Tom, horses is prey animals with their eyes on the sides of their heads, not in front like ours...we's been made like predators. Since they's prey not predator and only see with one eye at a time, the unusual odor of blood gits 'em skittish.

"Maybe Andy's team also sensed Jake and Absalom's nervous 'ague,' or somethin' different in the behavior of Alex Mcleod. Horses don't like snakes in the grass either."

"I asked Andy about the spellin' of Jaxton, and if'n he was indeed named after our former President. He said one of the comments from President Jackson, often quoted by Andy's family in reference to the spellin' they gave him was, 'It's a "blankety-blank" poor mind which can't think of at least two ways to spell any word.'

132

"So it was The President and me pondered different ways to spell 'murder.' We come up with four: 'm-e-r-d-e-r, m-e-r-d-u-r, m-u-r-d-u-r, and m-u-r-d-e-r.' We sposed we could include an 'h' and write 'm-e-h-r, or 'm-u-h-r.' However yuh write it, Tom, the crime is still the same.

"Because of no physical evidence of his involvement, and because Thornton had Mcleod's 'Jake-Abs' blurt, and because Andy was calm and cooperative from the get-go, our sheriff released The President, but, as a precaution, bonded him to stick around fer the hearin'.

"I think Andrew deeply regretted not pickin' up on the evil sooner. If he'd noted more concernin' Mcleod's character, he mighta side-stepped the stay with Uncle Henry, and thus avoided his cousins' involvement.

"Andrew said all he could think about was what he said to Abs after the boy mentioned 'We was out findin' a girl, and we asked her for...' Andy said what he said like he wanted to soothe his own conscience. He said, 'I told Ab he should never infringe on anyone's rights that way! I told him!"

CHAPTER 24 — SUNDAY, JUNE 30, 1872

The mourning dove issued a plightful call for rain. Its mate answered, "Coo, coo-oo, ah-cooooo." The two chimed their chant for moisture in dissident harmony.

Tom carried in another bucket. Phil said, "Seeing them bubbles pop sure does help me tell this story…"

The old man poured himself another glass of water, took a long drink, and swallowed with a louder gulp than usual.

"A week had passed. It was standin'room only at church. The congregation was wet with both sweat and sorrow. Durin' the service, Fred and the other farmers gleaned steam from St. Paul in the readin' from Galatians. Paul wrote in sharp and almost vulgar words, 'I could wish that those who trouble you would even cut themselves off…'

"Fred thought farm thoughts. *Castration might just be the answer*, though he knew the scripture was talkin' about the early church's arguments over circumcision.

"The next readin', also from Galatians, was prob-ly chosen to do double duty fer the upcomin' fourth of July, and the horror of gist a week ago."

Still wearin' his scratched spectacles, Duck Legs decided to find the verses. He picked up a tattered old Bible and, with remarkable speed, located the passage.

'Stand fast therefore in the liberty by which Christ has made us free, and do not be entangled in the yoke of bondage...for all the law is fulfilled in this, you shall love your neighbor as yourself'."

Phil added, "My version has always been 'Be polite to others, and good to yourself.' I like havin' gist one rule." Duck Legs put down the Holy Book.

CHAPTER 25 — THE HEARING

Yellow mustard flowers laced the fields. Red clovers provided a savory roadside munch and exuded their subtle fragrance. Early cornflowers contributed an occasional touch of tranquil blue. Thistles bristled midst the serenity, awaiting the next breeze.

Phil reopened his diary. He looked at a page close to the front and read to himself for awhile, seemingly to refresh his memory.

"Been waitin' on yuh!" Tom teased Phil.

"I've found it now, Tom. There's no time got wasted before they begun the hearin'. The sky registered red. I'll bet yuh know the sayin', 'Evenin' red and mornin' grey sends the traveler on his way. Evenin' grey and mornin' red, sends the traveler back to bed?' Some uses the sailors' version with 'mornin' and 'warnin'.'"

Tom nodded in recognition, averting more conversation to speed the story along.

"Though this was the farm-way of forecastin', no one went 'back to bed.' Fred was at John's finishin' the morning chores when he heard the barn door creak behind him. Then he heard John's voice. 'I know I shouldn't be surprised it's been you in my barn so early every morning doing my work. You're the best friend and neighbor a man could ever have. I don't know how either of us can farm without the other, but I have something I have to tell you.

'Probably Kate has mentioned how much Sarah is still in shock. She only leaves the kitchen to sleep. All day long, she sits at the table and stares at Belle's slate. She doesn't ever talk. It's like she's waiting for Mary to come home. I think the only way for the two of us to survive is to move to new territory. We'll wait until fall harvest is finished. They say it's beautiful in southern Ohio.'

Fred hung up the hay fork. He walked over to John and put his hand on his friend's shoulder. 'I understand. You can't function here anymore. The rest of us are having trouble, too. Kate and I would follow you if we could, but we can't afford to leave. The land of my dreams is full of nightmares now.'

"Fred figured it'd take about an hour for them to reach the courthouse. He wanted to arrive before the process was set to begin. Great Grandma came over to watch the children. Kate said, 'We plan to be home around noon. Someone told Fred hearings only last a half hour to two hours at the most. All the law has to do is present enough evidence to prove the need for a trial. They've notified John and Sarah they will be called to testify. I sure do wish they didn't have to reopen their wounds in public'."

"Three judges presided over the hearin'. When J. H. Day wrote his famous version, he only talked about one and called him 'Judge Lynch.' I'll call the one our sheriff knew best 'Judge Lynch.'

"The magistrate's legal history haunted him in a condescendin' way. He told Thornton, "Sometimes I wonder if my family will ever escape the law and go into another profession." His honor's digestive system touted his inner turmoil.

"The judge tried to be fair and meet the code of justice. But in a case this emotionally challengin', the code became the test of a lifetime.

"In his long career, Lynch had made many serious decisions. He owned a lot of law books. He studied hard, but

138

he never encountered as much pressure as he did in the blistery summer of 1872. Lynch knew he needed to detach from sentiment and reside in the letter of the law. Put in more common language, he had to snuff out his heart and think legal jargon, but he found he wasn't able to do nothin' about his stomach.

"The hearin' proved to be the most swelterin' ever. People said, 'It's hotter than Hades!' With the stiflin' conditions, the judge confessed to Thornton he'd experienced embarrassin' dreams about presidin' in his birthday suit.

"The courtroom overcrowded with folks who rode in from farther than the state line and sweat all the way creatin' what Lynch come to think of as 'farmer fumes.' The scent consisted of human perspiration, horse manure, and some splashes of equine urine. The women wore cheap fragrances, attemptin' to coat the other smells. The mix gist added to the confusion.

"The judge posted a large nose. It partnered with his sizable and sensitive stomach. His wife provided him with a sachet of lavender to put under his bench…a man had to do what a man had to do. He tried tuckin' the fancy bag of scent away where no one would notice. He kept a pitcher of water on the bench and a glass. He collected a small supply of peppermint leaves from his wife's garden to settle his innards. Lynch closed his heart in every way possible, so's he could be objective, but his ticker had attitudes of its own. Those attitudes dropped straight down and nested in his gigantic belly."

Duck Legs alternated hands to tap his own body parts and caught his fingers in the triangles of his suspenders as he spoke.

"Havin' the unsettled abdomen, unsettled mind, and an unsettled courtroom would soon make 'strike three' fer Judge Lynch."

"Grandpa Strouse was the first called to testify. Maybe it was good for him to get it over with. It wasn't easy, but even bein' a pacifist, he was upset enough to speak out loud and clear.

'We understand you were the last person other than the murderer to see Mary alive. Please tell the court how far away she was when you lost sight of her.'

'I could still see Mary at nearly three-fourths of a mile. I watched her to within fifty or seventy-five yards from where they found her body.'

"Strouse wanted to add the part about who left church early, but the prosecutor didn't ask more.

"Steen testified next. He was the one who'd found Belle's jaw and the back of her skull. He told how they left her parts lay 'til a jury of six men did the inquest. He also told about her pink dress and the belt.

"Dr. Wilson revealed the details of the partial examination he performed on site. He said, 'Her head was entirely off of her body.' He said, 'I believe a sharp object was used. I found human bite marks on her fingers, and the curved indents of fingernails on her neck and breast.'

"Sarah leaned forward, coverin' her face with both her hands and screamed, 'No! No! No!' John led her out of the courtroom.

"Each witness told the same details about where the body had been found in relation to Tama Road.

"Dr. Miller testified for the five physicians who did the exhumation on Wednesday. He used science terms to tell the names of each missin' bone. He said, 'About one-third of the bones on the head and face were gone.'

The prosecutor asked, 'What do you believe happened to the back of her skull?'

'I'm sure a heavy instrument of some kind destroyed the skull in the back.'

"The doctor had the exact measurements for the size of all of her bruises and went through those. Believe me, his testimony took a lot of time. He told precisely in inches where all the fingernail marks was found. People believed him with all the science and all, but with so many technical terms, like 'splenoid', and all them numbers, heads was spinnin'.

"Dr. Jones was next. He said, 'I found traces of blood on a limb. The skull fracture was consistent with a clubbing. There is no doubt Mary's death was the result of violence. Her neck had been cut. Most likely the person who did this would have blood on his clothing.'

"In cross examination, the defense shrewdly got Dr. Jones to admit there is 'an exception to every rule.' I'll read you his exact words. 'The perpetrator might have been able to avoid gettin' stained dependin' on his position when he severed her head, though this was unlikely.'

"After these five had had their say, the judge took a break. John and Sarah returned to the courtroom. 'The prosecution calls John Sitterley.'

'How old was Mary at the time of the murder?'

"Holdin' back tears, John said, 'Mary Belle's exact age at the time of the murder was thirteen years, two months, and twenty-six days.'

"No one had asked him to be so precise. The prosecution displayed her tattered and soiled pink dress. By then, most everyone was in tears. They asked John to identify it, which he did. They asked where her Testament and her parasol was found. He told, 'They were in the side ditch.' They asked the

142

distance of the church from their home. John said, 'The church is 'over two and one-half miles from our house.'

"John looked straight at the defendents and added without bein' asked, 'Henry's house is only a few rods over a mile and a half from the place of her murder.' His final words were not striken from the record. Fred heard the pain and anger in his best friend's voice.

"The next five laid groundwork fer the lack of alibis for each of the accused. To support John, they also pointed out the easy access to the murder site from Henry's house. It was noted, 'Someone can go all the way under the cover of trees except for when they cross the road right next to Henry's.' The deer had made trails.

"Mr. Smitley was called. He told about Mcleod and Abs leavin' church early. Grandpa Strouse nodded. He didn't need more evidence.

"Next it was reported how the accused departed at the crack of dawn on Monday mornin', and how they headed south to Jay City instead of north to Ft. Wayne, perhaps to throw anyone off who might attempt to follow if someone found the body. Early from church. Early from Henry's. The 'earlies' was addin' up.

"Deputy Johnson was called regardin' the details of the arrests. He told about finding the green ribbon tied to Mcleod's bridle.

"He also described the peddler's squirrelly behavior on the trip home from Ft. Wayne, and how his 'slips of the tongue' matched up with the crime.

"Johnson stated, 'Mcleod wasn't told the reason for his arrest until after we left Henry's, so up until then he wouldn't have known a "girl" had been "hurt" unless he was directly involved.' As an afterthought, he added, 'Mcleod and none of the other four were intoxicated when they were arrested.'

"Being sober was the only favorable condition the defense could point to, but it wasn't a strong point cause being drunk would have supported Mcleod's words was unreliable regardin' his memory of bein' innocent.

"The prosecution called Maggie Shepherd to tell about sellin' Sarah the bonnet and the ribbon. They asked who else bought the No. 9 green ribbon and where they lived."

Duck Legs paused for a long time. Tom turned to check on him. D.L. guessed his janitor wondered if he'd died during the telling. Phil stared at his diary. He forced himself to continue.

'The prosecution calls Sarah Sitterley to the stand.'

"An officer of the court guided Sarah to the front of the room. She looked frail and disheveled. People whispered how much someone can change in just a week. Neighbors and friends worried, thinkin' she might pass out from the ordeal, especially after hearin' about the decapitation. The spectators observed John wasn't a lot better off, but since Sarah was the one who knowed about the ribbon, she had to report.

"The prosecution promised they'd make the questions as easy as possible. Other 'n her name, and her relationship to the deceased, they only asked two.

"Producin' a rumpled green object, the lead prosecutor asked, 'Mrs. Sitterley, is this the kind of ribbon you purchased for Mary's bonnet at Maggie's store?'

"Lowerin' her head to hide her tears, Sarah nodded, then answered weakly. The judge had to repeat Sarah's answer so's everyone could hear, sayin', 'The witness has answered "yes".'

The prosecutor lifted the ribbon fer all to see. 'This is the same ribbon Deputy Bill Moore retrieved from the bridle belonging to the tin peddler, Alexander Mcleod'."

"The courtroom gasped.

'Was Mary wearin' her bonnet with this type of ribbon when she left for Liberty Church on Sunday morning, June 23rd, 1872?'

"Sarah fetched another 'Yes.'

'Thank you, Mrs. Sitterley. You may step down.'

"The prosecutor added, 'Like a head-hunter who saves the head, or natives who take a scalp, this savage took his trophy from the victim's neck. It's indicative of how various creatures from the animal world celebrate their kill.'

"Sarah had been the fourteenth witness. Andrew Jaxton was number fifteen. The hearin' wasn't lastin' two hours. It looked to be takin' the whole week.

"The President testified for a long time. I've got a couple of pages worth here. I'll condense it…

"Andy told how he and Mcleod arrived at his Uncle's on Friday, and the rest I already explained so's I'll spare yuh a repeat. I wrapped it up pretty good, if I do say so myself.

"On the other hand, Fred was beginning to wonder if the law would ever wrap up their presentation. So far most all they'd done was talk about the horrible details, the span of time, the location, the dress, and the ribbon. People wondered if the ribbon and Mcleod's bloody clothes was the only evidence the prosecutor had."

Deputy D.L. needed a trip to the latrine. Tom took a break as well.

Tom had returned to work and moved the ladder several times before Phil toddled back.

"Sorry 'bout the delay. Yuh probably thought I'd gone to the hereafter, but I had a ketch in my git-a-long."

In spite of the lapse, Phil was not one bit confused concerning where he'd left off. Sometimes Phil read as though he might be reading from the court transcript itself. Tom figured the deputy had a copy of it, too.

"The sixteenth witness was sixteen, but no sweet surprise: 'The prosecution calls George to the stand.'

"An accuse-eed didn't usually witness for the accuse-ers. The prosecution chose George because they expected him to give the same statement he'd rendered to Dan and Bill. George's testimony was secondhand, but they figured what he said would be enough to get the judge to declare the need for a trial.

Again, Duck Legs read word for word:

"George placed his hand on the Bible. The bailiff questioned, 'Do you swear to tell the truth, the whole truth, and nothing but the truth, so help you, God?'

'I do. I was home on Sunday with Andy. Mcleod was at the house nearly all day. He was not off the place. I had no conversation with Absalom or Mcleod about murderin' the girl.'

"Givin' the prosecution no breaks to ask questions, George's response sounded memorized. And, to the prosecution's dismay, it was the complete opposite of what he'd said on Saturday. However, the biggest problem with George's testimony was Mr. Smitley had gist told, under oath, how Mcleod and Absalom had attended church on Sunday, so obviously Mcleod was 'off the place.' Maybe George hadn't heard Mr. Smitley because he'd been busy practicin' what he was about to say. With George's obvious miskabobble, the prosecution lost all the ground they'd hoped to gain."

"Under cross examination, George told his defense attorney, 'I lied to Deputy Dan and Deputy Bill in the picnic woods on Saturday. I was afraid they would kill me unless I told somethin', so I told them that Ab and Mcleod told me they "had all the fun they wanted with the girl" and afterward killed her. All I told Dan and Johnson was a lie to get rid of them. I never had heard the story before but made it up as I went along. I told them I saw blood on Mcleod's shirt. That part was no lie. I did see blood on his shirt. That was true, and it was true that they washed at the pump.' He spoke without takin' a breath., so's to allow no questions in the midst of his response,
like he was primin' a pump in a hurry to git water. He only slowed at the end, finishin' with the elevated pitch of a school boy's recitation.

"The spectators wondered, 'Why summon George when, of course, he'd support the defense'?"

"The judge ordered a break. The hearin' still wasn't over. Fred and Kate wouldn't travel home 'til late. Great Grandma would feed the children and put them to bed if needed. This weren't the problem. The problem was all the work waitin' on them and every other farmer and farm wife in the shadow of the summer soltice.

"George would prove to be the complete undoin' of any kind of order in Lynch's court. 'Seems a lie always stirs us up like nothin' else can. The people was glad when George left the stand. Dan and Bill was glad. The red-faced prosecution was glad. Even the defense was glad. The judge's stomach fer-certain was relieved.

"No one benefited much from George's testimony, least of all George. His nervousness was more contagious than the typhoid."

CHAPTER 26—HEARING ANY MORE?

Some days the sky appears bigger than on others. It stretches like a giant balloon. Some days the leaves rustle louder, the brooks flow faster, but people don't have the time to notice the scent of flowers.

"Globby clumps of tension hung in the atmosphere way worse than the humidity. After his sticky examination, George grew even more fidgety.

"Fred could see how Jay City and a large portion of the rest of the testimonies was part of the evidence, but he couldn't understand why so much detail was bein' presented during the hearing. Fred thought, *Only the major physical evidence should come now. Circumstantial revelations should be left for later. Definitely, the prosecution should never have called George to the stand.* Fred believed the prosecution had 'put the cart before the horse, maybe several carts thinking one horse could push them.

"Questions floated during the break about whether more items might exist than the ribbon and blood on Mcleod's clothin'. Fred questioned, 'If additional incriminating items were found, why didn't the prosecution begin with a testimony from the sheriff who could have presented them?' Fred thought even if the law didn't want to begin with all of the evidence, a good time to present more would have been right after Sarah identified the ribbon, and they revealed Mcleod had tied it to his horse's bridle. The sheriff would have added to the momentum by showing other objects. Since this didn't happen, Fred commented, 'It appears all the exhibits have been presented.'

CHAPTER 27 — WEDNESDAY, JULY 3, 1872

*A slight breeze temporarily softened the air. Its miniscule flow
made the smallest leaves bounce in the emerging light of day
as if they were nodding "yes." Eventually, the atmosphere
built up enough force to send the tree branches into a united
horizontal sway as if they were saying, "No, no, no."*

When Tom returned, Deputy D.L. began. "It was the day before Independence Day, but no one was truly free. The July humidity formed a liquid prison, holding everyone hostage, chargin' equal fines, and punishin' us all the same.

"Once more Fred and Kate 'rose at four a.m. They hurried through mornin' chores and left a little after six, hopeful the hearin' would conclude before the holiday. Fred told Kate, 'I think the sheriff might be called today. I can't believe how long and drawn-out this hearing is. I wish the legal community knew we have work to do. I guess the man who claimed it wouldn't take more than two hours had no notion about how the law operates. We can only farm when the crop clock says it's time. Now it's nearly past time.'

"Then Fred did somethin' unconventional.   He snapped at Kate. 'It would have helped today go better if you hadn't burned our breakfast.'

"Neither of 'em spoke as they traveled to the trial.

"The prosecution began with, 'We call Sheriff Thornton to the stand.'

"Thornton was also impatient. He'd mentioned right before he left, 'Presenting these items first might have made for one day in the courtroom instead of three.'

"Though not under any 'crop clock,' maybe the prosecutors had begun to think the same, 'cause they instructed Thornton, 'Please show the court all of the remaining evidence.'

"Slowly and carefully, Thornton unwrapped the first item. It was a pen knife with a sizeable blade. He'd showed it to me the day of the arrests. Over fifty years later, I kin still see the dried blood. The knife hadn't been used to sharpen quill pens unless the owner was usin' blood fer ink.

'Raise the weapon high, Sheriff, for the court to view. Now please tell us when and from whom you got this object.'

'I took this knife from Alexander Mcleod when I arrested him on Friday, June 28th, 1872.'

"A gasp interrupted the sheriff. When George saw it, he gasped, too. Maybe he visioned the cuttin' of Mary's neck, and thought how her blood had sprayed. I know it's what happened to me.

"No doubt it made him recall the red splotches on Mcleod's shirt, and the huckster's desperate scrubs to remove them. Maybe he thought about the woods, and bein' there with the deputies while the pigs rested in their wallow.

"George stopped fidgetin'. The boy sat motionless, starin' at the bloody knife, almost like he'd been the one stabbed.

"One evenin', back in the jail, George had told me about a bad injury. It happened when he was little. It bled for a long time. George had said, 'I've always hated the sight of blood.'

'The prosecutor continued, 'I believe, Sheriff, you have another item to show the court.'

"Thornton unwrapped the second object. He said, 'This also belonged to Alexander Mcleod. I took it from him when I arrested him last Friday.'

"It was a handkerchief. Unlike the knife, it had only tiny specks of blood, barely visible from a distance. Even Lynch had to squint to see them. Some wondered why the sheriff bothered presentin' it. But George knew why. Even more than

154

the knife, the kerchief stirred somethin' inside of him. He jumped from his seat, rudely interruptin' the sheriff and announced, 'I need to get back on the stand! I have something to say. I need to say it now!'

'Cause of his response, the neck George needed to save promised to be his own. No one ever butted in on a sheriff's testimony at a hearing, let alone demanded to replace him.

"Judge Lynch immediately called both the prosecution and the defense to the bench. The prosecution argued, 'We request George be allowed to return to the stand. We have called both George and the sheriff as our witnesses, and since we are still calling the witnesses, it gives us the right.'

"The defense disagreed. Their lawyer, Callen, stated, 'George can't just interrupt the sheriff and be the one to proclaim he can testify again. If the prosecution wants him as a witness, he can be recalled once the sheriff is done presenting his evidence, and we've had the chance to cross examine.'

"This is what Callen said, but I'm guessin' what Callen thought was, *I'll bet George is going to change his story. If we can bargain for more time, maybe I can get him to shut his trap.*

"The judge hesitated fer what seemed like a country mile, then ruled, 'The motion by the prosecution is sustained.

Sheriff, you may step down. Take the stand, George. You've already been sworn in. No need to repeat the process.'

"His honor struck his gavel. George, who'd been standin' the whole time and shifting from leg to leg, appeared google-eyed. He all but leaped forward, leavin' the defense speechless.

"Sheriff Thornton carefully folded the handkerchief and passed it to the balif.

Comments corralled the courtroom:

'I can't believe the judge allowed anyone to interrupt our sheriff when we were finally seeing the evidence.'

'Why is he letting George have two testimonies when Sheriff Thornton hasn't even finished one?'

"Lynch commanded, 'Order in the court! I demand order in the court!'

"Thornton didn't resist the judge's rulin' even though he wanted to add, 'In my mind, this second piece of evidence is one of the best we found.'

"Too bad the court didn't get to hear Thornton, but I guess with what happened next, they didn't need to."

CHAPTER 28 – GEORGE AGAIN

Grey streaks cut through the clouds in parallel rows as though an angel plowed furrows through a discolored sky.

"Before yuh hear George's second efforts, Tom, I need some fuel in my furnace. I saved two cookies. I'll share."

After they'd finished eating, and Deputy D. L. had brushed the crumbs from his stubbly chin, he resumed. "It's too bad George didn't have his watch to note the exact minute he retook the hot seat. This time the details made him more believable, as did somethin' different about his mannerisms. This time George wasn't gist sayin' a piece fer a recital, he was givin' himself some peace."

Phil adjusted his spectacles to read George's testimony: 'On Sunday, June 23rd, at about 3 o'clock p.m., Mcleod told me that he struck and killed the girl. That he first had all the fun he wanted. He said Absalom was with him. There was blood on Mcleod's shirt, and he washed it off at the pump.

Mcleod told me these things when he and I were trading watch chains. We were upstairs on a bed.'

"George told others later how he'd hatched his idea fer the swap while he waited on the peddler, Jake, and Abs to return from their jaunt through the woods. George figured he could upgrade his own links, which was constructed of an even cheaper metal than his watch. Though his wasn't as fancy, his was sturdier. He'd use durability as his bargainin' point.

"George reasoned an item once belongin' to the tin peddler would be an interestin' draw fer conversation. It might even help him git noticed by a girl. He planned to pull it out of his pocket and say, 'I bartered long and hard to get this from Alexander Mcleod. It at least came all the way from the city of Ft. Wayne... maybe from even farther north, since Mcleod hailed from Canada, you know.'

"George checked the hour as he and the huckster mounted the stairs. Seems nobody questions the time as much as the owner of a new watch. George figured opening it in front of the peddler would seem like the idea fer the exchange had gist occurred..."

'Hey, Alice, I mean Alex, how about swapin' chains?'

'Yes!'

"George did a double take. Had Mcleod just agreed? Strangely, the peddler seemed eager and hadn't responded to his tease. George had risked hearin' 'Gee-orge' to get his attention.

"Mcleod sat on the bed. Mcleod had pockets deep enough to hide stuff. In the left, he kept his watch and handkerchief, in the right his billfold and knife. George could see the tip of a handkerchief when Mcleod pulled out the watch. George was surprised about the length of the chain—so much had remained unseen. The peddler removed his watch. He handed over the chain almost like he couldn't wait to make the trade. Since George had expected the peddler who traded fer rags to drive a hard bargain, he felt a surge of disappointment. He'd have no yarn to spin about how long he had to haggle.

"Mcleod immediately attached George's cheap chain. His mind was loaded with other matters. The bedroom was dark. All the curtains had been drawn to keep out the afternoon sun. Mcleod musta felt safe in a place with no light where his shadow didn't show. Sittin' on the bed, in an eerie, braggin'-kinda voice, the peddler spoke the incriminatory lines George quoted both in the woods and durin' this, his final testimony: 'I had all the fun I wanted with a girl, then I struck her so she wouldn't tell. I think I mighta' killed her.'

"George couldn't believe what he heard. He'd never forgit the words. It explained the blood. George shoved his new-got possession into his pocket. He'd traded watch chains with a murderer. He didn't touch or look at it fer the rest of the day. He vowed he'd never put it on his timepiece.

"George squirmed on the witness stand. Images of Mcleod stabbin' Mary in her breast and cuttin' off her head caroused in his mind, danglin' like Mary's head must have dangled.

"George described later how he caught the scent of a hog wallow and could feel trickles of somethin' warm runnin' down his forehead. He wondered if the drops was red.

"Thirteen-year-old Mary was only a few grades behind George in their one-room school. He remembered her well. He'd prayed a few benches ahead of her at Friend's Church. He recalled when her mama died. A surge of sadness moistened his fear. Then the fear became strong enough to prompt George to say somethin' about why he lied. 'The reason I told a different story when I was first examined was because you lawyers told me to go back on what I had told…'

"The lawyers fer the defense quickly backpedaled. All three attested, 'George told us he "made certain declarations that weren't true." We advised him not to repeat these under oath.'

"Whatever situation existed between George and his lawyers, all the arguing ceased, and the defense said, 'We have no further testimony.'

"Lynch released George at noon on Wednesday, July the third, in time fer him to celebrate double freedoms.

160

"Then Lynch called for a break. To the sheriff's surprise, during their time off, Absalom decided he'd confess, too. Perhaps George goin' first give him a safety net.

"When court resumed, the prosecution submitted Absalom's words to the bench whereupon the defense objected. They questioned whether Thornton had forced Absalom into his guilty plea durin' the break with no acceptable legals around to verify it. And, although not mentioned, overtones regardin' Absalom's capabilities rung like a dinner bell. The defense wasn't beyond tryin' every angle since not one of their defendants had an alibi, or a single scrap of evidence in their favor, or against anyone else. They'd lost their only hope, George. If Lynch accepted Absalom's admission of guilt, all options fer evadin' a trial had most likely vanished.

"After much debate, the judge ruled, 'The court will not allow Absalom's testimony.'

"A lot of the observers, includin' Fred, reasoned, 'I thought this was a free country. Doesn't his honor remember tomorrow is the founding day of our freedom? Shouldn't everyone be allowed to have their say?'

"Others shook their heads. 'Twice for George, but not once for Absalom.'

"Lynch thought he'd formed a valid choice, but the rural and city folks didn't agree. Uproars surfaced. The farmers and the locals couldn't understand. They felt Ab's comments should have been presented, after which, the truth could be considered.

"Poundin' his gavel, in a hoarse voice, Lynch screamed, 'Order in the court!'

"It was the judge's worst nightmare to have a room of spectators he couldn't control. He'd completed the first phase of what would become a recurrin' theme. His honor had made the minority happy...everyone else found 'emselves furious. The judge didn't care what others thought, so why did his stomach care? He put some mint into his glass of stale water and took a big gulp. He choked on a dry leaf. Ready for the day to end, Lynch announced, 'Jake's exam is postponed until after the Fourth.'

CHAPTER 29 — JULY 4, 1872

On the Fourth of July, the emergin' white lace of the wild carrots, the red clover, and a sparse sample of blue displayed the nation's colors. They were the only patriotic blooms on Tama Road.

"Choosin' to avoid public comment, Henry's family stayed home on the Fourth. George told later how he decided, *When I can get the money together, I'll buy myself a new chain. This one was in the same pocket as Mcleod's handkerchief. If specks of Mary's blood made it through to the handkerchief, I'll bet her blood is on these links.*

"George brought it close to his eyes for inspection, and then angrily hurled it into a pile of trash. No wonder Mcleod didn't hesitate to trade with me. 'Bet he thought if I had a watch chain with blood on it, I'd look like the guilty one. He'd use his nosebleed excuse, claim I had the chain all along, point the blame at me, and be long gone.

"George primed the pump and scrubbed his hands over and over in case any blood lingered on his fingertips. Then, bendin' over, he put his lips to the stream of water fer a long, cold drink. As he swallowed, George noticed someone had removed the tin cup, which had rested upside down on the notch of the spout. The cup was Mcleod's gift to Henry's family fer his stay, 'a token,' Mcleod had said, 'for my room and board.' George thought, it was indeed 'a token.' It wouldn't surprise me if Mcleod took it before he left.

"George clenched his fist and jumped onto the fence to watch the cornstalks sway in the wind. He needed some moments of quiet to calm down. I'm guessin' he didn't bother to check the time."

Thornton thoughts matched George's. He told me, 'The handkerchief is as important as the bloody knife, because it has so little blood, an obvious disproof of Mcleod's nosebleed excuse. Surely anyone with a nose-bleed problem would have more on their kerchief. My theory is this cloth remained in Mcleod's pant's pocket durin' the murder. The specks soaked through when he severed her neck due to the untimely force of her last heartbeat. Those tiny dots of blood are Mary's, not Mcleod's.'

"Thornton said he'd planned to hold the kerchief high in the air fer the courtroom to see, gist like he had the knife. The sheriff joked with me privately, 'Do you suppose Mcleod will say he used his knife to pick his nose and that's how the blade got bloody? Maybe he'll claim he accidently grabbed it to stop his nosebleed instead of his handkerchief. Or perhaps he'll claim the feather was full of blood when he used the pen knife to sharpen the quill, even though no quills have blood in the hollow, and most every one uses dip pens now.'

"I heard Thornton confront the peddler right after they returned from the hearin'. 'Too much blood on your knife, too little on your handkerchief. Weigh the evidence against your nosebleed excuse, Mcleod.'

"I'd have overlooked the kerchief, but not Thornton. He was tuned into every detail. Thornton, Andy, George, and I agreed. It weren't a nosebleed.

CHAPTER 30--JAILBIRDS

The owl sat sharp-eyed on the fence, feathers camouflaging all but the glare in his eyes.

"From the get-go, I was the full-time guard while Thornton split his time between the court proceedin's and his crops. Our sheriff was as stressed about his harvest as Fred and the rest of the farmers who had counted on justice.

"I was somewhat familiar with Henry's boys since their pa had been in the house a year ago. I got the inklin' Henry woulda made a great writer or artist, but farmin' gist wasn't his passion. With over a dozen mouths to feed, Henry didn't have much choice but to stick with a plow. It was rumored he drank some on the side, prob'ly to hide his pain. I suspected hard cider coulda been involved when he got arrested fer assaultin' the elderly man.

"Now let me tell yuh about Absalom. I felt real sorry fer the boy. Usually I called him Abs. He didn't have a clue about how this all happened to him. He cried 'most constant in his cell.

"I never did figure out why he was named after King David's son from the Bible, since he appeared the total opposite—nothin' to look at, not smart, and, fer certain, not royal. I didn't believe Abs committed the murder but figured he mighta committed rape after someone showed him how.

"I never saw no one weep like he did. He reminded me of a little boy in a grownup body. I didn't try to mask my deformities around him. I knew I was far better off 'n he'd ever be.

"It didn't surprise me when the judge threw out his confession on the grounds he was induced to confess. We all knew the trouble he had talkin'. A fine line existed between helpin' him say what he meant and actually givin' him the words. We finally learned it often worked best to ask him questions with 'yea' or 'nay' answers.

"After George's release, I was down to three jailbirds accused of the murder...Abs, Jake, and Mcleod. Jake stayed to himself. He appeared shy and scared. Seldom did he give me more 'n a nod of his head. Them two brothers was no trouble at all.'

"Alexander Mcleod, though, as I've said, showed himself to be a different part of the horse's body. He was some hawker of wares, all right. Mcleod proved to be unpredictable. He reminded me of a teeter totter. I began to refer to him privately as 'Teet.' The word can mean 'utter' things, too, yuh know."

Tom laughed and almost spilled more suds. Phil said, "Don't be dumpin' yer bubbles, now."

"At first, Teet claimed complete innocence. He was so charmin' and convincin', at times even I almost believed him. He had a strange habit of smoothin' his eyebrows after he claimed it wasn't him, then he'd rub his nose and chin or the side of his neck— 'never did figure him out.

"One day, out of the clear blue, it looked as if he'd confess. His voice sounded friendly. 'Get me some paper….', he said. I waddled back as fast as I could with the paper, a dip pen…even our jail used dip pens…and an ink bottle. Whereupon he looked me straight in the eye and said, 'What did you bring these for? I never you asked for writing materials.'

"Mcleod had blue eyes. Most times, blue eyes is pretty, but his was the ugliest I ever did see. They squinted out from under his curly mop of auburn hair. I'm bettin' he didn't go to no barber. It occurred to me he gist put one of them tin bowls over his head and hacked away with a dull scissors, prob'bly also made of tin, if there is such a thing.

"Around Mcleod, I felt unsteady, both motionally and e-motionally. After he lied to me about the confession, I couldn't help but think I, too, might be in danger of gettin' chopped.

"George's disruption of Thornton's testimony became fodder fer jailhouse cud-chewin'. We began a discussion about unpredictable people. I decided to rank our prisoners. I ranked 'em from the most predictable to the least. Abs scored the best, then Jake. Even though he'd been released, I included George as third. Teet came in last."

"The Fourth passed with only an undercurrent of the usual hoopla. People found 'emselves too devastated to commemorate a holiday. Closeness to our nation's one hundredth birthday did git noticed. Half-hearted comments was made about 'We need to think ahead fer the centennial,' as if to give people somethin' to look forward to though the only serious plans bein' made was of a totally different kind."

CHAPTER 31 – FRED AND KATE ON THE FOURTH

No breaks formed amidst the clouds. They completely frosted the domed sky.

Tom was ready to begin another wall. By now his fingers resembled prunes and matched the color of his soapy bubbles. Tom said, "My wife might think if I can wash walls at the Infirmary, I can help her with the dishes."

Duck Legs said, "Yuh better be findin' yourself a pair of gloves to hide them wrinkles. Best leave 'em on 'til after your wife gits the dishes done."

Old Phil removed his spectacles. "Now let me tell yuh how it was with Fred 'n Kate on the fourth. Their nerves was as parched as the soil. Kate's feelin's still hurt from Fred's comments about her burnin' breakfast. Both of 'em was touchy. John and Sarah wasn't the only ones not talkin'. In states of total exhaustion, they struggled to catch up with the wheat, hay, straw, and household chores with no free moments fer celebratin'. Not that they wanted to anyway.

"While Kate burned their food, Fred neglected puttin' his tools back where they belonged. As big as it was, he even misplaced his scythe. He found it leanin' against the back of the barn where he'd left it late the night before. Little specks of rust had formed where dew-drenched grass had touched it. Fred kicked his barn. The scythe toppled sideways.

"Fear and fatigue form the wrong kinda fertilizer, yuh know. Sayin' Fred was bone-tired was an understatement. He'd have preferred clearin' eighty acres of timber any day over this.

"More'n losin' patience with Kate and himself, Fred was losin' patience with the law. Like I said, Tom, 'Those who ain't patient won't never be kind.'

"Fred told my pa about a nightmare he had featurin' empty fields with no grain to harvest. Weeds grew instead of wheat. Then in the same dream, he saw his broad ax broken at the neck. The break was jagged. All remainin' on the wooden shaft was a small pitted and rusted piece of iron. The biggest part of the blade lay separate. Because the break was uneven, repair looked impossible.

"Most of Fred's dreams still centered on makin' coffins. His newest featured four in a row. Instead of bein' tiny, they was normal-sized in length and width, but they was deep, so deep Fred couldn't see the bottoms. He wasn't able to tell who was inside without leanin' over the edges and nearly fallin' in himself.

"One by one, Fred identified the occupants of the first three as Phebe, Anton, and Baby Emma. He peered into the fourth. It was the deepest…like a cave. The image blurred. Fred had to hold down a lantern. When he saw Kate's lifeless form, it was about too much fer him. Her head was detached. Her blood coated the cushion."

CHAPTER 32 — FRIDAY, JULY 5TH, 1872

The clouds resembled spilled popcorn. Heaven told its story in puffy paragraphs.

Tom wanted a break, but knew he needed to keep working. Perhaps he could loosen the stiffness in his arms and neck by moving them in circles. His bosses had suggested the timetable of a room a day. The young custodian determined he'd finish Deputy D. L.'s before going home even if he had to work late. It would be worth it to hear the end of the story. Tom sensed something was about to change.

"To the surprise of everyone, on Friday, July fifth, the prosecution said, 'All of the state's evidence has been presented. We rest our case.'

"Addin' to the stale air in the stiflin' room, the spectators breathed sighs of relief. Though the judge knew the farmers reserved the custom of bathin' for Saturday nights. Judge

Lynch wished exceptions could be made when they attended court. The farmer smell hadn't gotten any better. The scent saturated the room, smotherin' all traces of the lavender he'd hidden under his bench. Periodically he squeezed the sachet, hopin' fer a fresh whif.

"Big green buzz flies found their way inside and dove without a pattern. Women's wrists ached, and fingers cramped from excessive fanning. In desperation, some of the men took up the practice and held flowered fans.

"On Friday, the courtroom became infested with a second surprise. After hearin' the openin' statement, Jake, the follower and shy one, decided to pull a George stunt. Jake had counted on the prosecution summonin' him. When they rested their case instead, he stood and complained, 'I was never called to testify!'

"He got an immediate response from his lawyers. 'We object! The prosecution has closed their case. We haven't opened ours. Neither side has called Jake as their witness.'

"The prosecution argued, 'We have rested our case, but because the defense hasn't begun theirs, we ask ours be reopened.'

"After a lengthy drink of water, the judge declared, 'The defense's objection is sustained. The court will not reopen the case for the prosecution. Jake is not granted testimony.' The judge slammed his gavel so hard, he was lucky the end didn't fly off and hit his big schnoz.

'Twice for George, but not once for Ab or Jake!' reverberated throughout the courtroom. Thornton said it sounded like what he'd heard called 'staccato' in music.

"People said, 'Obviously common sense doesn't rule here, and from what we can see, there's very little democracy.'

"The general public concluded the decision would keep Jake from ever testifyin', just as Absalom never got to testify, and Thornton never got to finish.

"Suspicions filled the room. The magistrate was as bewilderin' and unpredictable as George and Jake. Attitudes sprouted in the form of, 'Our law reeks with unreliability.'

"With all the indecisive wranglin', a sense of 'here we go again' festered amidst the people, and nothin' short of full-force pandemonium erupted. The description I'm goin' to read is from J. H. Day..."

Duck Legs picked up a little brown booklet with an engraving of Mary on the front and an engraving of Absalom and Jake on the back. The deputy turned a page and read, 'The whole audience arose as one man and commenced closing in toward the place where the prisoners sat...Women (were)...so scared of violence...they hurriedly (left) the courtroom. Men

175

were cussing. Forty or fifty men storm(ed) out and head(ed) for the jail.'

Then Deputy D. L. paused. Removing his spectacles, he said, "Maybe the line between innocence and guilt had melted in the summer sun. It was hard to tell with all the cryin', and accusin' and disclaimin'. The law only knows about guilty and not guilty. It don't know nothin' about love and fear."

CHAPTER 33 — ORDER

More flies buzzed nonstop. More humidity…when would the temperature drop?

"No denyin' it, Tom. 'Order in the court' convulsed with every slam of the judge's gavel. As Lynch yelled his demands, the raps on his bench rebounded in his stomach.

"Finally, Thornton had to restore the decorum since his honor couldn't. Suddenly the sweaty magistrate changed course and said, 'Call Jake to the stand.'

The tall one took the oath, then said, 'Mcleod confessed the murder to me today at noon.'

"Jake musta reckoned the judge could be swayed by sayin' a specific time, like happened with George and the tradin' of the watch chain. With what seemed to be a nod toward helpin' his older brother, Jake added, 'Mcleod forced Absalom's involvement.'

"Jake said nothin' about rape. Neither side questioned him regardin' it. Everyone wanted the hearin' to be over."

"As Jake hoped, Judge Lynch released him, too, then adjourned fer the day, makin'no mention of whether he'd rule in favor of sending the case to trial.

"The community was aghast over setting half of the prisoners free, and equally steamed about the predicted two-hour hearin' continuin' into yet another week. Lynch was releasin' the suspects and incarceratin' their harvest.

"The bloody knife, clothin', and eerie possession of Mary's ribbon sure seemed like more than 'beyond a doubt' to Fred and the others. Although, Tom, is anythin' 'midst humans 'beyond a doubt?' The word 'reasonable' had done slid out of everyones' vocabulary.

"Seein' the state of her husband's distress, Lynch's wife sent lavender, mint, and now chamomile. The judge added the powdered chamomile to his stale, mint-flavored water. He downed the mixture, leavin' the glass empty. He and Thornton exited through the back door, whereupon the judge lurched forward. A circle of vomit landed on his protrudin' stomach.

"As Fred untied their horse from the courthouse hitchin' post, he said to Kate, "I'd swear I can smell the packet ship."

CHAPTER 34 – THE WEEKEND

Enveloped by a cloud of resistance, people tried to find their way.

Tom began work on the fourth wall. Mindlessly spinning his spectacles on the bedside table, Deputy D.L. stared at the rainbows bouncing off the surface of the bubbles in Tom's galvenized bucket.

Phil said, "I'll tell yuh now about how it was over the weekend. The dates was Saturday, July sixth, and Sunday, July the seventh, thirteen and fourteen days after Mary's murder. Yep, two weeks had passed, but fer the most of us, it seemed like two years. Unrest, uncertainty, and unbelievable fatique tornadoed their wide paths down Tama Road. Who knew what direction the storms might take? Fer sure, everyone had put up their emergency sails followin' Jake's release.

"Sheriff Thornton was concerned about the disasters springin' up in the courtroom. Because fifty-some men arrived when I was alone on Friday, Thornton decided to batten down the hatches. He barred the jailhouse door from the inside.

"Thornton told us deps, 'I'm getting a little too much help from my farmer friends. Rumors are rotating they might confiscate our prisoners and dispose of them.'

"With the front door nailed shut, I reckoned I'd become a jailbird, too. Occasionally, I st-st-stuttered when I spoke. I remember sayin' to Thornton, 'Whoever h-h-heard of l-l-lockin' people out of j-j-jail? Some c-c-celebration of f-f-freedom this t-t-turned out to be.' I hoped no one would notice and say I sounded like I was qu-qu-quackin'.

This time, Tom couldn't help himself. He let out a hearty laugh. He hoped he hadn't hurt the deputy's feelings, but Deputy D.L. chuckled, too.

"As you'd expect, Friday's courtroom antics caused the revision of my predictability list. I now chose to rank George and Jake together in a brotherly tie second place from the bottom. Judge Lynch, come in gist above them, though I considered switchin' their placin's. Abs remained at the top as most dependable. Teet trailed as least.

"Here, Tom, have a look fer yourself."

Deputy Duck Legs held his diary out to his janitor. Tom quickly dried his hands on his pants to accept it.

The diary read, "Most predictable to least....

Absalom

Judge Lynch

George and Jake

Alexander Mcleod.

Other option:

Absalom

George and Jake

Judge Lynch

Alexander Mcleod

"I decided I'd keep both lists. I'd run 'em by our sheriff, who, since he'd actually been at the hearing, could be more objective. He surprised me by showin' his first sign of indecisiveness, whereupon I nearly added Thornton to the list, right above Abs, of course.

"After a long pause, Sheriff T. said, 'My recommendation is give two placings instead of four. Put George, Jake, Lynch, and Mcleod all on the same line. Nobody on your list has been consistent except Abs.'

"I said, 'Well, I 'most always agree with you, Thornton, but not this time. In my mind, Teet's definitely the bottom feeder.

The best argument I kin come up with fer your argument is 'being unpredictable is Mcleod's only predictable trait.'

"My new list read:

1. Absalom

2. Judge Lynch, George, and Jake

3.Teet'."

CHAPTER 35 — SATURDAY, JULY 6, 1872

The moon appeared like an iridescent comma in a black paragraph. Surrounded by sentences not written in straight lines, the paragraph was punctuated with periods made of salty stars.

"Come Saturday, another strikin'ly orange sunrise blossomed in the eastern sky. Although in late afternoon or evening, Saturday was traditionally a goin'-to-town day, no one in the community was travelin' anywhere after the gruelin' week they'd spent at the hearin'. Wheat, hay, and straw awaited someone to harvest them. Berries and beans needed pickin', bread needed bakin'. Houses needed cleanin'. Bank loans needed to be paid, if only they could.

"In spite of the stress, the Tama Road community in their straw hats and big-rimmed, feed-sack bonnets did take the time to gossip over split rail fences, makin' comments like: 'This stuff about who can or can't testify is mish-mash. All of the boys arrested should be allowed their turn.

'If the judge agrees enough evidence exists fer a trial, I heard the location might change. I heard it might be moved all the way to Ft. Wayne in hopes of finding an impartial jury. How will they git witnesses to come if they move it there? We'll lose our harvests for sure if we're called to testify and have to travel so far every day. It's impossible. We can't afford it, and our horses' hooves couldn't take it either.'

"Others added, 'No matter where they hold the trial, "beyond a shadow of a doubt" is sure to be used, and they might all go free. Then where would we be?'

'Yah. Especially if Mcleod continues to claim he's innocent, and Absalom isn't allowed to speak. They're the only two left.'

'If "shadow-of-a-doubt" happens, and the huckster goes free, no one will be safe around here, or anywhere else he travels.'

'They've let two of the four go already. Nothin' would surprise me now.'

'If the hearing was supposed to take a few hours, but took the whole week and still isn't over, can you think how long a trial will take?'

'It's too hot to be sittin' in a stinkin' courtroom. I think I kin smell myself in the next county.'

184

'Yah. Way too much time in our fields has been lost. We can't afford to spend our whole farming season confined in Lynch's territory. Our crops looked good early-on, but the wheat I take in now will get docked for mold. Much longer and the stalks will go down. Grain will fall out of the heads. We'll be crawling on our hands and knees trying to salvage what we can. For sure, I won't be able make my farm payment then.'

'We're all in the same boat. Enough has been sacrificed already by those on Tama Road when we lost Mary. We shouldn't be the ones imprisoned in a courtroom and forced into giving up even more.'

"A remark by Grandpa Strouse made its way around the community: 'I remember what George Washington said in regard to our Constitution. He said, "Its only keepers (are) the people'."

CHAPTER 36 — SCRAGGLY, SCORCHED, AND DENTED

The summer has its own schedule.

"Fred's beard grew scraggly. In his effort to take care of everythin' else, he neglected himself. With two weeks lost to the tragedy and the legal misfirings, he hadn't had enough daylight to hoe one weed. His fields matched his chin. Fred had cut acres of native timber, but now he couldn't muster the time to chop a few hairs or weeds. Some Canadee thistles began to go to seed.

"To top it off, as Fred hurried down the haymow ladder at John's, he stepped on an uneven spot on the dirt floor of the barn and wrenched his ankle. Don't git ideas, Tom. It didn't help him git out of work.

"Fred limped back to their cabin. He asked Kate fer an old cloth. She tore one from her wedding dress. After they'd married, she'd worn it to church for several years, and then for everyday, cookin', cleanin' house, and workin' in the garden til it couldn't be patched anymore. Now, she tore the once pretty skirt into long skinny strips. She handed one to Fred. He recognized it. He looked longingly into her clear blue eyes. Then he wrapped the fabric tight around his ankle. He grabbed a piece of bark out of a crock on an open shelf and chewed, hopin' to ease the pain.

'Haste makes waste,' he told Kate as he winced to his feet. 'By the way, I'm sorry I complained about the burnt food. It's a miracle either of us has gotten anything accomplished these past two weeks. Tears formed in Kate's eyes.'

"Though Kate tried hard for Phebe's sake, her cookin' wasn't up to snuff. She spent much time scrapin' scorched bits off the bottoms of pans she forgot to stir. She had burns on her fingertips and the palms of her hand. She was distracted—not like herself at all. Her only singin' was lullabies.

"And, as was to be expected, nothin' at all had begun to heal for John and Sarah Sitterley. Unless someone stopped by, neither of them spoke inside or outside their beautiful dwellin'. Every bit of their energy was consumed in wadin' through the deep waters of sorrow and anger. Fer the first time in his life, John didn't show much interest in his work. Sarah didn't even try. Dishes piled high in the dry sink. Their kitchen smelled of rotten food. Sarah neglected to comb her hair. Everyone understood.

"Back at the jail, I overheard Teet tell Abs, 'If others had kept their mouths as closed as I did mine, no one would have known anything about it.'

"The peddler was already caught in not one, but two webs, one spun by George and the other by Jake…well, three webs, if you count the evidence, and four if you count what Absalom wanted to say, and five if you count the huckster's own slips of the tongue.

"Right away, I relayed Mcleod's blame-filled comment so's Thornton could record it. I wanted to be sure our spider was permanently caught in his own web.

"Thornton said, 'Thanks, D. L. Teet's never officially confessed, but he admits his guilt in many ways. I'll keep making a list of his blunders. When I get the chance to testify again, I'm going to present my full copy. The tin peddlers got enough dents in his ware now, added together, they just might stand as a full confession of Mary's murder. For sure, the defense will have to work overtime to persuade anyone to think otherwise.

"A little later, Mcleod summoned me again. He asked me to bring paper, pen, and ink. He even said, 'Please.' In an apparent change of heart, and with as much charm as he could muster, he added, 'This time, I will write out a full confession.'

"I found these words a little more convincin' than the first time he talked me into bringin' the writin' materials. Maybe Thornton wouldn't need the jail's 'full copy' after all. Words written in Mcleod's own hand should be considered 'beyond a doubt.'

"No sooner had I reached through the bars than Teet, who could never admit anythin' was his fault, or stand any criticism, denied he'd asked fer the materials and denied sayin' he'd give a 'full confession.'

"I questioned Thornton, 'How old is Teet anyway? I think he's got hardenin' of the arteries or hardenin' of the somethin'. 'Funny how he used the words 'full confession.' We have over a week's worth of partial ones from him. Your 'full copy' is gittin' gist as long as his 'full confession' mighta been. Yuh know, Thornton, given how fast the varmint forgits, maybe we should locate a cell for him down there with the insane. Fer sure his thoughts is constipated. I'll dip his bread in Castor Oil.'

"The next skin-pricklin' words was a statement about his mother. She seemed to be the one keepin' him from the 'full confession,'

Deputy Phil adjusted his spectacles. I'll read it for yuh. 'My mother taught me to do better, and it would break her heart if she knew I was guilty. The last words to be carried to my mother shall be "I am innocent".'

"I said to Thornton, 'If she knew I was guilty!' He's finally admitted it! But how kin a woman in Canada, or wherever the heck she is, possibly be controllin' her twenty-some-year-old son way down here? I never saw strings pulled from that far."

CHAPTER 37 — JULY 7, 1872

A haze hovered over the fields causing hallucinating distortions. The pervasive mist united the farm community in its steamy ether.

"It was Sunday, July the seventh, exactly two weeks to the day after Mary's murder. Because of Friday's uproar, Thornton chose not to leave the jail fer his usual weekend at home.

"Gist as the sheriff passed Mcleod's cell, Teet reached through the iron bars and grabbed Thornton's hand. Thornton jerked loose since the huckster couldn't git a firm grip.

"Teet said, 'I never meant to say that you or anyone else testified falsely against me. I know I said so, but it was only from the lips out and did not work from the bottom of my heart.'

"I remember how Thornton stared directly into those steely blue eyes. He never give Mcleod the courtesy of a reply.

"It was the wordiest, flowery-est, awkwardest apology Thornton had ever heard, even from his seven children. Most was about Mcleod, without any direct 'I'm sorry' to the sheriff. As far as I was concerned, it confirmed the peddler's position on my list.

"After Teet's display, I teased Thornton, 'I'm gonna tell Jane you was holdin' hands with a prisoner.' Thornton didn't laugh.

"In private, we tried translatin' what Mcleod said and did into 'What was he really sayin?'

"Thornton said, 'I think this was his way of believing he could control me both physically and mentally. He must have thought *If I grab hold of your hand, I'll grab your attention and get some control of your mind.* Did you notice, D. L., how he seized me from behind just like he did Mary?'

'I did, and I'm wonderin' why you think he said what he said about never meaning to say what he said?'

"'Who knows? It's easy to get stuck in Mcleod's muddy words. My guess is it's a part of his 'I'm innocent' yarn. He seems to think saying, 'I didn't mean to say…' makes him not guilty. And so does the part about his "lips only" and not his heart. He might think if he said it with his "lips only," it wasn't a lie, but he fibs to himself. I figure he used the same strategy with his mysterious mother. It's something a child would do.

192

Maybe Mcleod actually hugged the woman in an attempt to gain power over her.'

"The thought made both of us cringe. Shortly after the hand-holdin', Mcleod added another barrel of unpredictability by callin' directly fer his sweetheart instead of me. I was real glad he hadn't asked fer me...I'd have brought the Castor Oil.

"Teet said to Thornton, 'I'm ready to give a confession'."

CHAPTER 38 — CONFESSION CONFUSION

The molten sun emblazoned the sky. Like the fire inside a giant kiln, it streaked the earth with an eerie yellow glaze.

More water slopped onto the floor. Tom found himself alternating between mopping it and washing the wall. He couldn't postpone clean-up, because the soapy water would constitute a slip hazard endangering both Phil and himself. Tom knew his messiness came from fatigue. He figured if he tackled both the wall and the floor with the same water, he'd have less refills.

"This is how our sheriff handled the new line of ware Mcleod peddled. He played hard to get.

'I'm busy right now. You've had plenty of time to confess. I'll be back later.'

"Waitin' wasn't somethin' the tinner was fond of. Teet didn't have much patience. Guess it's why he had trouble findin' ways to be kind.

"Thornton delayed, not only because he needed to add Mcleod's new twist to the list, but also to show the huckster he wasn't the one in charge though he seemed to think he should be.

"Mcleod said, 'You're just like my mother. She was too busy, too.' Then the peddler stared at his hand like babies do when they first find it. He looked in particular at the long fingernails on his left hand. He flicked them nervously with his right thumb nail. Click. Click. Click.

"The jail chaplain had given him a Bible. When he calmed down, Teet said to Abs. 'While I wait, I'll see what the the Good Book says about murderers.'

"I watched him open to Genesis. What Mcleod read seemed to startle him. His mother had ignored him. The sheriff had refused to hear his confession. Now, he was readin' words that recognized his nature.

"His skin flushed till it reflected the color of his hair. Sweat run down his ruddy cheeks. His eyes looked small, misplaced, and sunken. He created a colorful picture against the cell's white-washed walls. Slumpin' over the Bible, he hunched to scan the pages. His frame went from one who'd been pouncin' to one who was gittin' pounced upon.

"I suspect Mcleod didn't read far before he recognized the patterns in his own life. I reread the first chapters so's I'd have an idea. Here's the points I think affected him.

"The first was Eve seemed the boss, gist like Teet's mysterious mother. Eve's the one who favored eatin' the apple, though all women's not pushy, yuh know, and men kin be the same way, too.

"The second, 'Cain was angry.'

"The third, 'Sin lies at the door', out of sight, waitin', like he'd hidden and waited before grabbin' Mary.

"Then I saw him stop readin' and stare. I figure it was when he spotted the words, 'Cain killed.'

"God questioned, 'What have you done now?'

"Yep, Alexander Mcleod's name coulda replaced Cain's in most all them sentences. God's response was familiar. Folks remembered he'd told at the railroad 'lection about his mother usin' the same words.

"I saw Teet glance left and right. Maybe he wondered if unbeknownst to him, she had arrived and was standin' at the door to his cell. Maybe he thought he heard her raspy voice, cuttin' and stabbin' his heart like a knife with the accusin' words, "What have you done now?

"Perhaps his nerves had become as speckled as his handkerchief. He mighta reasoned, *I thought I silenced my*

196

mother's voice forever when I sliced a female throat and stabbed a breast. I think all he wanted was to injure a female, any female, to revenge his mum.

"Cain's territory was familiar. I could see it from my desk. The tin peddler was back in the hive with the queen bee on attack. He was the prey he vowed not to be.

"He seemed to sense physical discomfort as he read. He placed his hand over his heart like he was the wounded one. He went back to readin'. I couldn't tell if he was about to laugh or cry."

"Here's the verse I think answered his question about God's response to murderers: 'The voice of blood cries...from the ground. So now you are cursed from the earth...a fugitive and a vagabond you shall be.'

"All the words applied.

"The part about 'cursed-from-the-earth' musta been the part he took as God's answer to anyone who killed. Bein' cursed and bein' forgiven's definitely at opposite ends of the rope, so to speak. I'm guessin' this is when Mcleod gave up hope. The Creator didn't have room here for murderers. It was right there in the Bible.

"If he'd kept readin', he'd have found evidence fer redemption, but instead Mcleod closed the cover with a slap like the one his controllin' mother probably used on his face.

197

He had his answer. He was 'cursed from the earth.' It mighta seemed, he'd always been.

"When Thornton returned, I remember the exact words Teet uttered. The sheriff wrote 'em down. I copied 'em.

"He told Thornton, 'I have made all the confession I am going to make, as there is no forgiveness for a murderer.'

CHAPTER 39 – THE PEDDLER'S NIGHTMARE

A ghost moon lingered.

Though Tom was pushing hard to finish, he found he had to stop and listen when Deputy D.L. remarked, "Let me tell yuh how it was when Teet had the nightmare. We all heard him scream. His voice sounded high-pitched and as shrill as a bobcat's.

"Since in Teet's mind his chance of bargainin' with God was over, the only glimmer of hope remainin' seemed to be to convince his mother he was innocent. When it came to God or man versus her, no toss-up about who he feared most existed. Teet had switched from bein' a predator back to bein' the prey of Mother Mcleod.

"I never did figure out why we think we have to be either either viscious or a victim. Both might not be us. Maybe we's a separate category all of our own, or maybe we is a blend.

"I watched Teet cry himself to sleep right before his nightmare. After, Abs asked, 'Why did you yell out in your sleep?'

"I was surprised when Mcleod told him: 'It was because a woman, who looked like my mother, stalked me on all fours. I crawled as fast as I could. She had her own face, but she had the body of a lion. Every so often, her head shifted into a furry outline, savage and snarling and roaring, teeth coated with saliva. I felt an object in my hand. I looked down. A green ribbon dangled in the dirt.

'The lioness yelled, "What have you done now?"

'Flames erupted ahead. The inferno didn't scare me. She was gaining ground. To stop her, I looked back and screamed, "I'm innocent!"

CHAPTER 40 — SLEEPING THROUGH THE SERMON

Signaling the approach of a storm, sometimes the atmosphere creates a shelf formed by a single cloud running for a long expanse of sky. Perhaps it's meant to be the area where we deposit our troubles in the hope the Creator will take care of them for us.

Phil watched Tom grab the dirty rag from his bucket, wring out the murky water, and attack more grime.

"The crop clock only had a short time left, Tom. It does not rewind. Meanwhile, it chimed louder than ever. On their only day of rest, the farmers on Tama Road felt the pressure.

"Still nursin' his sprained ankle, which throbbed when he walked, Fred only had time for a quick glance in the mirror before they headed to the Reformed Church. The image lookin' back wasn't one he recognized.

"Fred admitted to sleepin' through much of the Sunday service, but he did remember the minister focused on Galatians. He heard the part about…Only one law, love your neighbor as yourself,' and found himself wishin' the legal community would pay attention…one law, treat everybody the same. Everyone is allowed to give a confession if they so choose, and let the sheriff finish his testimony.

"But how could Mcleod be considered a neighbor worth loving when he'd murdered a neighbor? Fred knew which neighbors he loved. He'd forgotten the parts about 'lovin' your enemies and those who hurt you.' Up to now, Fred hadn't had any enemies.

"The preacher continued, 'And those who are Christ's have crucified the flesh with its passions and desires…' A lot was spoken about flesh versus spirit. When Fred dozed off, the message faded. 'Only one law…' he heard in his semi-conscious state. Unfortunately, 'love your neighbor' blended right into 'crucify the flesh with its passion…' In his state of exhaustion and pain, the plug of reason had been pulled. The struggle fer survival was gittin' the best of him. Fear took over. Gist like in the Garden of Eden, the snake hissed: *What if the judge releases all of the accused because of 'shadow of a doubt?' No one will be safe with rapists and a killer or killers at large. Two of the four have already been let go.*

The final point of the preacher's sermon was also from Galatians. The minister said, 'The flip side of the love-your-neighbor coin applies to both humans and animals. The tail's side of the coin, get it, Tom? The tail's side reads, 'If you bite, you'll get bitten in return.' Them two verses are back to back in Galatians. It's like verse 5:14 is fer people, and 5:15 is fer our animal or untamed side. I got 'em right here. I'll read 'em to you...

'For all the law is fulfilled in one word, even in this; Thou shalt love thy neighbor as thyself.' And here's verse fifteen... 'But if ye bite and devour one another, take heed that ye be not consumed one of another.'

"Notice how it says not gist 'get bit,' but 'consumed,' like we did the cookies.

"Some more of what Fred seemed to miss the preacher say was, 'When we're tame, we don't act like animals, and we don't find the need to bite each other.'

"The minister talked about how Jesus said in the Sermon on the Mount, 'Blessed are the meek, for they'll inherit the earth.' He told about the Greek word for 'meek.' He'd mentioned it the previous Sunday, too, and so had the leader at Liberty Chapel...they must have been talkin'. He said the Greek, or Hebrew, or one of them languages, word for 'meek' is 'p-r-a-e-i-s.' I wrote it down so's I'd remember. Maybe it's 'p-r-a-e-u-s' or 'p-r-a-u-s.' I'm havin' a little trouble readin' my writin'.'"

The deputy adjusted his spectacles. "Anyway, the preacher said the word could have been translated 'tame.' The preacher even said he thought it was a shame it got transcribed as meek, which can be like tame, but has a more sheepish take in our English language. Yep, he actually said he suspected what Jesus intended was fer us to stop actin' like animals who tear each other apart, then git torn-up in return. Them cycles always repeats and repeats and repeats. He proclaimed those who are tame 'will inherit the earth.'

"Another interestin' tidbit is a small town gist a short ways to the east with a railway station is called Tamah, pronounced the same, spelled different. 'Tamah' is an old Indian word meanin' 'innocent'?

"I've wondered how bein' tamed and bein' innocent is connected. I remember Jesus sayin', 'Except ye become like little children…' I like to think we's innocent first, when we's babies, and not out gist fer ourselves. Hopefully, when we become out fer ourselves we do get tamed, so's those of us who do will 'inherit the earth.' In German, the passage with the word 'praeis' would read we'd be 'heirs to Erden'."

"Some of the men met briefly after church. They said, 'This isn't somethin' to be discussed on Sunday. Let's leave early Monday morning. We'll ride into town on horseback. We'll meet at the fairgrounds and form our plans.'

"The men from Indiana who attended Fred's church promised to join 'em. They said, 'Indiana's laws aren't as strict as Ohio's. Hoosiers have gotten away with this before. We'll do the work.'

"Fred wasn't sure what they implied was a good idea, but he didn't have a better one. Since many of the group was older, he decided to rely on their judgment.

"My mother remembered how the church women held their own conference:

'Look at the men all huddled together, whispering. I get the feeling they're up to no good.'

"Kate responded, 'Fred's been up to no good all week—not like himself at all. First, he was grouchy because I burned our breakfast, then I saw him hit old Baldy and yell at him. I've never seen him hard-spank any of our horses. It's just not like Fred. Poor Baldy turned his big head to look at Fred as if he was asking "Who's behind me? It can't be you, Fred!" He put his big ears back and hung his head...Horses have feelings, too.'

"My mom tried to console Kate. 'We're all upset and not ourselves. Everything and everyone is out of place everywhere on Tama Road'."

CHAPTER 41 — THE TEARS OF ABSALOM

The connections that reside in coincidences are the
heartstrings of life.

Tom had never heard the word praeus or praus. He'd never thought much about humans being made like an animal predator with eyes front and center and canine teeth, as well as like prey, with molars in the back, sharp teeth and flat, and how our animal side needed taming even though we weren't like other animals cause of our language, hands, and the way we walk. He considered we might be, as Lincoln had implied, something different, "a little less than the angels."

Tom's dad had served in World War I. From seeing the effects fighting had on his pa, he knew too much of the side of the beast existed in war. After returning, his dad suffered signs of shell shock...signs of having been 'bitten' and 'biting in return.' Tom had witnessed his dad's bouts with depression, and his volatile temper, and the fears that made him scream at night, too. Tom's mom had said, "Your dad was never like this until after he returned from the war."

Tom hoped what the verse said about 'the tame inheriting the earth' would somehow, someday come true. He thought, *Little children get punished for biting. Why is it allowed in other ways when we become adults?*

Deputy D. L. continued. "It was on Sunday, July seventh, when Abs quit cryin' long enough to relive the events of the two prior weeks. First, he recalled the railroad election and the booze. He remembered prayin' in church when midway through Mcleod decided to leave, and said, 'Come with me.'

"Abs was glad to get out of a hot, stuffy building, and a crowded pew, and into the open air. Mcleod promised him, 'I'll show you a new kind of fun. It'll be better 'n booze. I'll help you get a girl.'

"Absalom had never had a girl swoon fer him in any way. He'd never seen 'em flutter their eyelashes gist fer him, nor had any come close enough to drop their hankies at the church socials. Most of 'em avoided him completely.

"Mcleod devised the plan. 'We'll get the girl on her way home from church. We'll hide in the bushes and take her by surprise.'

"Absalom liked surprises. He thought the girl would, too.

"The brown-haired girl with the pretty eyes and freckles posted a large bosom. It was all Abs could think about. He didn't know how he smelled after the night of drinkin' at the railroad 'lection. His hair stood up and out and was an oily yellow. It was more than a week since he'd bathed, but he didn't care. He wasn't worried about what the girl thought, at least not at the time. He was focused on gettin' her. It was something men did.

"People had teased and bullied him his whole life. He knew he was different. He didn't know what the horrible word 'retard' meant, but he knew it weren't good. He figured it had somethin' to do with him not being able to read or write. Though he couldn't form his name, he could, with effort, draw an X.

"Yep, Abs had so little of which he could be proud. He was proud of makin' the X. He could build things. He could say his complete name and the names of his whole family. He considered these as two. Now he wanted to be proud of 'havin' a girl.' He counted five items. It was a big moment in his life. Henry and Andrew saw Ab touch and retouch each digit. They told later how they didn't know what he was doin' and didn't bother askin' since he was odd by their standards. He appeared to be tallyin' something. Abs had always been better at cipherin' than he was with words.

"However, gettin' his fifth accomplishment didn't go as Absalom supposed it might. Mcleod led the process, but not in a good way. They ran across the road and hurried down the deer path. They waited. They could hear her comin'. She stopped by the orange lilies. Mcleod came from behind. He grabbed her and scared her. Abs saw how terrified she was. Bein' frightened was never somethin' he liked to have happen to himself or anyone else. She screamed for help—no surprised happiness in her face.

"Absalom might not understand a lot, but he understood emotions. He didn't need fancy language to recognize 'em. Love and hate, and was it calm and fear? It didn't sound right. Abs changed it to 'afraid and unafraid.' Something and anger...was it calm? Calm seemed a lot like love to Abs. People kept tellin' him to 'Stay calm.' Were anger and fear alike, too? Abs couldn't come up with the opposite fer anger. Fer him, it was gist anger. There was happiness and sadness. He tried to remember others, but nothin' else come to mind. Feelings seemed to erupt more from his body and heart than from his head, anyway.

"He saw the fear in Mary's eyes. Anger flooded Mcleod's. Abs thought the peddler would be happy. What was with his mean eyes? He remembered the peddler had promised this would 'be more fun than booze.' So far, it wasn't any fun at all.

"Mcleod took his turn first, then Jake, and, as always, Abs was the last one included, except Mcleod took another turn, makin' himself both the first and the last. Abs said when Mcleod begun and when he finished, he laughed."

"Absalom's feelin's wasn't happiness, or fear, or anger. Instead, Abs felt sad fer what they was doin' to Mary. He remembered her name. As he copulated, he sensed the stiffness and repulsion in her small body. Seein' her betrayed felt familiar. He wasn't proud of 'having a girl' after all.

"Though sometimes Abs didn't grasp the whole conversation, he understood the part he heard later about how Mcleod returned to kill her 'so she wouldn't tell.' And he remembered Mcleod had warned both himself and Jake, 'You keep your mouths shut!' He figured out what would happen to them if they told.

"He remembered seein' Mcleod become like a vicious dog, growlin', his teeth barred, his gums, tongue, and the veins in his throat showin', the kind of animal no one could trust.

"Henry overheard Mcleod's 'keep your mouths shut' comment. I'm guessin' Abs smiled ear to ear when his pa said, 'You can't go to Ft. Wayne with Alexander Mcleod'."

"By Sunday evenin', our two remainin' prisoners was discussin' the community outrage. They'd seen and heard Thornton bar the jailhouse door. Suddenly the air hopped with the business of confessin'.

"Usually by eleven everyone snoozed soundly, but not on July 7th, 1872. I told Thornton, 'It's definitely not lucky 7-7-72, even if three sevens is in the date'."

"Twice, Abs requested to give another confession. I wondered if maybe he heard Mcleod use the word, and thought if Teet fessed up first, it was safe fer him to follow. Probably he thought the truth would set him free like it had George and Jake. Did he understand the court refused his first statement? All I knew fer sure was Abs was still cryin' back in his cell.

"I said to the sheriff, 'I'd take Abs pen and paper, but a whole page of X's won't tell us anythin'.

"It bein' Sunday, Thornton found it difficult to track down an authority to record Ab's words. Our sheriff wasn't about to take the boy's confession without one and risk a second accusation of coercion and a second denial of Ab's testimony.

"Thornton needed to locate someone who could translate Abs thoughts to paper in a readable and legal fashion. But apparently, all of the big-wigs was takin' Sunday naps after their fine Sunday dinners or visitin' friends or relatives.

"The sheriff said, 'We'd best dig up a dignitary so this document stands.'

"I loved the phrase, 'dig up a dignitary.' It was the best laugh I'd had all day. I couldn't resist askin', 'Where we gonna stick the shovel?'

CHAPTER 42 – ABS SPEAKS AND THE LAW LISTENS

The night air had a ghostly ring. It amplified every vagrant sound and intensified every odor.

"Here is what the shovel dug up, though it was a long time scoopin'. Judge Blake didn't arrive until eleven p.m. Thank goodness Absalom still wanted to confess. We could depend on him."

Phil picked up his diary, and slid his glasses back up his nose to read Ab's words:

'I, Absalom...of my own free will, do make the following confession, to-wit. While we were going through the woods on Sunday, June 23rd, 1872, from church, Mr. Mcleod said, "Let us go a squirrel hunting." I told him we had no caps, that John Ricker lost them all on Saturday. Nothing more said until Jacob. . .came home, then Mcleod asked Jake if any girls went west, and Jake told him that several went, and Mcleod said: "We will go out there." We then ran the greater part of the way. When we got to the spot where the murder was committed, she…was within one hundred yards or more of us, and when she came up even with the place, he, Mcleod, stepped out and said, "Hold on," when she ran to the south side of the road and hollered "Let me loose" in a loud tone of voice. He then grabbed her by the throat and right arm and took her behind the bushes and threw her down. We, Jacob and myself, were off about two rods when Mcleod called for us to come there. We did not go until he called us the second time; we then went to him and Jake stood at the roadside to watch and I at the north of the girl and Mcleod, when Mcleod told me to take hold of her arm, which I did. At that time Mcleod was holding both of the girl's hands in his mouth…the palms of the hands together…holding to her throat. Mcleod had connection with her. I then watched until Jake had connection with her also and then Jake watched until I did the same thing, then Jake and I went off about twenty-five yards, when Mcleod again had connection with her and as soon as he was through, he picked up a club and hit her on the head. The club was about four inches in diameter and three feet long. I saw her throw up her hands and quiver when he struck her. He then came running up to us and said that he had knocked her in the head. We then ran home. I saw blood on his right wristband and also on the bosom of his shirt. When we got home, I ran into the barn, Jake went into the house, and Mcleod washed himself at the horse trough and afterward washed again at the pump, and then went into the house, and all ate dinner. About 1 o'clock and at about 6, we went to water the horses (myself, Jake, Andy, and George), and when we came back, I met my brother Sam at the crossroads, and jumped with a lot of boys. We then went home at sundown and a little after we ate supper. Mcleod told me that he had been back there and (she) was not dead yet, but that he had killed her. On Monday morning my father told me that Alex wanted me to run off, but he wanted me to stick to the clearing'." His mark X. Absalom…

Attest: R.G. Blake, Sheriff Thornton, Deputy Dan…"

"It was a lengthy confession 'cause when Abs was short on words, Judge Blake asked him a lot of questions, like 'From here to where was the distance?' and 'Show me how big the club was,' and 'Did George mention the approximate time? And 'What happened next?' Then Blake would enter the information. Often, he phrased the question so Abs could answer 'yea' or 'nay,' or he gave him choices of what to answer, like 'Which would you say it was closer to, the building next door or the one across the street?' It took an hour to complete. When Abs signed his X, it was near midnight. I had had enough for one Sunday, and so had everyone else. I told Thornton, 'It would be nice to start the new week with my eyes open.'

"As I put my head to the pillow, I noticed an unfamiliar silence.

"I planned on sleepin' well since both Thornton and Deputy Dan stayed over. However, because Abs had mentioned Jake's involvement, and the judge had freed Jake on Friday, and everyone implicated needed to be in the slammer, middle of the night or not, this was yet another job fer Sheriff Thornton and Deputy Dan.

"The sheriff said, 'Waiting until morning will be too risky.' Thornton wanted to be back by dawn. Too much was brewin'. He and Dan hitched the wagon and rode into the darkness on yet another lengthy trek, leavin' me alone with the prison population, locked in like an inmate, only the entire buildin' was my cell.

"Thornton's departin' words was, 'Bar the door as soon as we leave.'

"After they'd gone, I got to thinkin' about the late dinner Abs had spoke of in his confession. George had mentioned it to me as well. George had said, 'When the plate of meat was passed, Mcleod took two pieces. Everyone else took only one, like usual. I was last to get it. When the platter reached me, it was empty'."

"At about three a.m., Thornton and Dan returned with Jake. By then I was deep in sleep. Thornton had to bang on the door several times to git my attention. They deposited Jake in the cell he'd left gist two days before.

"I remember how the tall one could barely bring himself to look at Abs. He'd learned the reason fer his re-arrest. I'm sure he wished his older brother knew how to lie.

"We all settled in fer what we hoped would be a couple of hours of much needed shut-eye. But snoozin' was a pipe dream. An hour later, around four a.m., a lot of commotion sizzled in the city. Well, back then it was gist a town, but I like the sound of 'sizzled in the city,' better, don't you?"

Tom nodded, but thought, *Come on, Phil. Finish the story!*

CHAPTER 43 — MONDAY, JULY 8, 1872

Mosquitoes swarmed in dark places, readying for their next meal.

"I see yer gettin' close to completin' your job, Tom. So am I. About one more bucket of suds oughta take care of both of us.

"I'll never forget how a few days earlier a crescent moon had slivered the sky. Floatin' on its point, the moon looked like a shiny boat tipped over on its bow. The farmers said it showed it pourin' out water. They'd need to git their harvestin' done before it rained.

"By Monday, July the eighth, the moon's phase had turned dark. Fred didn't sleep well. His ankle pained when he moved. He awakened at two-thirty, roused by a new dream. This time it featured a mob of howlin' k'eye-oats, some calls 'em coyotes. They was new to the Midwest, comin' in from the prairie as forests was cleared and livestock was raised. The state didn't record an official citin' in Columbus 'til 1919, but we'd seen a few of 'em along the Indiana/Ohio state line back in the seventies. Prairie grew on the west side of Indiana, yuh know. They didn't have far to go to reach us. Them officials was always a little behind.

"In Fred's dream, the k'eye-oats ran rampant, killin' everythin' in sight. The lead k'eye-oat turned its head. Fred recognized its face. It was Mcleod.

"As Fred left the cabin, Kate said, 'I'm worried. Be careful.'

"Fred told her, 'I'm not taking my gun.'

"She handed him a large slice of beef jerky and his leather canteen, which she'd filled with fresh water. Their blue eyes locked gazes. I'm bettin' he kissed her good-by, 'cause no children was up to watch his display of affection.

"Fred left his weapon in case she needed it, since, as far as he knew, two was set free, and lived mighty close. Many of the farmer's wouldn't be takin' theirs fer the same reasons.

"Fred headed to the barn. He readied their drivin' horse, not fer a trip by buggy, but fer a ride on horseback, which the men at church agreed was faster and would allow fer a quick get-away if needed."

"He thought he heard a k'eye-oat howl in the distance. It reminded him of his dream. Fred's instincts fer survival told him they was doin' right. Mcleod should be treated like the animal he'd become. Fred's mind saw the k'eye-oat clear as day, but Fred's heart saw Mary, Phebe, Anton, Emma, and Kate, and all the remainin' children and women on Tama Road. He juggled his head and heart thoughts, mixin' em like oil and water.

"Though tired and in some pain, Fred rode on, sourcin' adrenalin as he joined the others in route, about two hundred of 'em when they reached the edge of town. As they neared their destination, Fred caught scent of a dead animal. It lingered in the mornin' mist.

"Kate couldn't sleep. She worked around the cabin, tryin' to keep herself busy and not wake the children. It was Monday. Laundry awaited. She gist wanted it done.

All of us at the jail heard the ruckus when the group arrived. When there's thunder, lightnin' can't be fer behind. Thornton double-barred the jailhouse door in the center. He fixed two smaller native timbers, one at the top and the other at the bottom. No one would go to the hearin'.

"By ten a.m., people packed the streets. The jig was up. The reason became clear around noon when nearly two hundred individuals, includin' those who'd met at the fairgrounds, rode up to our jail on horseback. A multitude of onlookers joined 'em on foot. The noise and dust invaded first.

"I worried the mob might be mean-spirited, but they didn't look threatenin'. They seemed calm and well-organized...no shootin' of pistols like we'd heard of out West, no cussin', screamin', rantin', or ravin' like from the courtroom bunch who visited on Friday but changed their minds about waitin' on the prisoners. Monday's visitors did, however, look dead-set on what they was doin'. Thornton and me recognized many. They was mostly farmers.

"The mob left their horses stand without tyin' 'em. 'Remarkable how well-trained them animals was. The men walked calmly to the jailhouse door. When they found it barred, one broke in through a window.

"Sheriff Thornton warned the intruder, 'You've broken a window, but that's not all you're breaking. You're breaking the law. This is government property. You don't want defacing it or illegal entry on your conscience or on your record. Taking up residence here will cost you both time and money. I'll serve a stiff fine fer what you've just done, and a daily jail fee as well. Don't put your livelihood in jeopardy. Let the law take its rightful course. But, if you repair the damage, I'll overlook this infraction.'

"As if the intruder heard nothin' Thornton had said, the man quickly freed the bars on the door and the others bolted in, as many as could get in, that is. They clearly outnumbered us. The sheriff was on equal ground in terms of strength and common sense with most of 'em, but not with the whole blessed group. It was not like him to give up, but he had no choice. Our posse weren't no match for a couple hundred muscled farmers.

"Thornton couldn't bring himself to pull his gun and shoot, 'cause many was his friends. He recognized others as the same ones he'd questioned about two weeks prior on Tama Road.

"After wrestlin' the sheriff and Dan to the floor, the farmer mob tied 'em up. They confiscated the keys to the cells. Thornton kept warnin' the group about the consequences, tryin' again to reason with 'em, but they wasn't listenin'. The group moved like a fine-tuned mantel piece, wound gist right, all gears tickin' in sync. They registered shock when they saw Jake. They thought he'd been set free, and they'd only have two to take.

"Jake and Abs cowered in their cells, while Mcleod stared at the mob, glassy-eyed, his blue marbles protrudin' from their sockets. The peddler tried to shame and blame the farmers with a desperate plea. Later Thornton recalled and recorded Teet's words. I got 'em right here. 'I'm innocent. Whatever you do to me, you will be doing to an innocent man. Your conscience won't forget your mistake today. You will break my mother's heart. I'm innocent.'

"Yep, he was a child alright, but this child weren't anywhere near tame. It was interestin' to see how he focused on his innocence and on breakin' his mother's heart, and tryin' 'poor me, you should be the ones ashamed.'

"I begun to wonder why I wasn't bein' bound. After all, I was a sworn deputy gist like Dan. But the mob only kept me cornered. Soon I learned the reason. They ordered me to hitch the wagon.

"I always knew I walked funny, but when my legs vibrated, I waddled even worse. I saw the knots the farmers used to tie Thornton and Dan. They wouldn't be gettin' loose any time soon. I cooperated, no questions asked.

"They led the trio from their cells. Teet was the last one released. He rasied his left hand to smooth his eyebrows and nervously stroked each several times before his cell was unlocked and they cuffed him. It was like he had to look good for this event. They forced the three into the wagon and shackled their legs. The farmers didn't have me do one bit of this work.

"Since I knew a lot of the men from Tama Road, I hoped Thornton wouldn't think I'd participated in plannin' the break-in, 'specially since they chose me to drive the wagon. But Thornton knew a lot of 'em, too. It's gist the way it is in a small community.

"The spokesman directed me to head toward the site of the murder. It was the longest, dustiest ride of my life. I worried the prisoners might turn on me and use me as a hostage fer their escape.

"Thankfully, Mcleod either hadn't thought about makin' a run fer it or he figured he couldn't pull it off with an escort of two hundred on horseback. What he was able to muster was a bloody nose. With his hands cuffed behind his back, Mcleod's only option was to bend forward and smack his schnozzle on the seat in front of him. He made it look like it happened 'cause of a bump in the road...a bump he knew was comin'. Some told later, they saw it happen.

"Many of those who'd stayed home in the mornin' now joined our circus train. When I glanced back, I couldn't begin to see the end of it. Newspapers reported there was thousands.

"I wondered the whole time if, with this heavy of a crowd, Mcleod would do some re-evaluatin' and confess. But instead, he talked freely, like he was the grand marshal of some

225

magnificent parade. No matter the situation, he seemed most happy when it was all about him.

"While at the fairgrounds, the mob made plans to lynch the prisoners at the exact spot where Mary was murdered…'an eye for an eye, and a tooth for a tooth,' they said. When we arrived, the owner stood at the edge of the woods, hands on his hips, waiting.

"He crossed his arms over his chest and said, 'I didn't give permission to use my property. There's already been one murder here. I don't want my soil tainted with three more.'

"The group was stymied. Everythin' had been carefully determined, even down to which tree to use. Their plan had its first flaw.

'We can't take 'em back to the jail.'

'We'll have to find a new spot.'

'Let's haul 'em across the state line…'

"Henry arrived. He overheard. As he listened, he musta found himself wantin' to save face. After all, three of the four originally arrested was his offspring and the fourth was a guest in his house when the murder occurred. How could he live in the community with this hangin' over his head, so to speak?

"Life fer Henry's family was unravelin' like giant spools of thread. The strands was gittin' more and more tangled. No one

226

could tell how to untangle 'em, 'specially not Henry. Life was unrollin' out of his control.

"The boys' yarns appeared grey...nothin' completely clear, no obvious black and white. The spools all had let loose close to the same time, but they conflicted...Henry, whose name meant 'home ruler,' couldn't rule.

"Henry looked like he was evaluatin' what he knew and searchin' fer the truth. I figure he sorted it out somethin' like this: *Andy was home with me all day and implicated Mcleod, Absalom, Jake, and George, but said he didn't want to include George.*

George's strands are the most tangled. He alternated between, 'Mcleod did it. He didn't do it,' and 'He did it.' George's strings do begin and end in the same place!

Jake only had one thread. It connects to Mcleod. Jake said, "Ab was forced by Mcleod. Mcleod admitted the murder to me at noon on Friday. I had nothin' to do with the murder."

I've been told Absalom has willingly confessed all three committed the rape. He said he was there when Mcleod used the club. He told the same story every chance he got. Yet his confession was denied in court, because the defense claimed his words, no matter how unswerving, were "induced by the authorities.'

227

Meanwhile Mcleod continues to claim he's innocent, but Andrew's, as well as all three of my boys' statements, and every piece of evidence point in his direction.

"It was Henry's last chance to rule. He made a spur-of-the-moment decision. 'Bring the wagon to my house. Lynch 'em there. Those who did this should be punished at home'."

"Jake and Abs heard everythin' their pa said.

"As directed, I turned the wagon back east. It weren't no easy turn-around on them ruts, and I had to cut through the crowd. The folks from aways back couldn't figure out what the heck was goin' on. I couldn't stop to explain. Eventually the word filtered through.

"At the corner, I headed north toward Henry's. The mob followed. Since the lynchin' had been planned fer the big woods, the farmers had nothin' at all in mind fer up at Henry's. Shortly, however, they found a spot straight out from the front window of his house. Henry's wife and all of his family, includin' George, stood by the window and watched."

Duck Legs paused long enough to cause Tom to stop his work to check on him. He thought old Phil's eyes looked misty.

D.L. resumed. "A giant oak grew on the property. The sturdiness of the tree begged its use. It was odd how the mob was so law-abin' they respected whether they could or couldn't use a man's land without permission but had no noticable qualms about stringin' lynch ropes.

"I could see George through the window. He checked his watch. I looked at mine. It was comin' on three o'clock, full into the highest heat of the July day.

"They had to hurry. The men improvised the gallows. They cut a saplin' and hoisted it into position, supportin' a limb of the oak. Leavin' their prisoners in the wagon, they instructed me to drive under to determine the height. They adjusted the fork on the one end to accommodate Jake. They made him stand to be sure they was correct. They strung three ropes, decidin' a slip knot would work gist fine. 'Cause of the unexpected delay, no one took the time fer the thirteen turns of the traditional noose. They couldn't chance bein' in process if authorities arrived.

"I could see a few strands of Jake's black hair had caught in the sisal rope when they checked the height, like a precursor of what was to come.

"Finally, when everythin' appeared ready, the spokesman addressed Teet.

'Alexander Mcleod, you've only got minutes to live. We understand you have yet to submit a formal statement, but you are the prime suspect in Mary's murder. All of the physical evidence points your way as do all of the testimonies. We're giving you one final chance to make peace with your Creator. Do you have any last words?'

"Though shackled, Mcleod wobbled to a stand and began his lengthy discourse. I have it right here, gist as J.H. Day recorded it."

Tom leaned forward. The young custodian figured with a rope ready, and the threat of what follows a broken neck being 'the great unknown,' the tin peddler would finally offer his "full confession."

Duck Legs read word for word from his diary:

'I am asked to make a confession. I cannot condemn my conscience. I know nothing of the transaction—never saw the girl in my life to my knowledge and never touched her. I did not commit the murder. I am innocent of that crime and know nothing whatever about it. (Henry's family) know I went to bed and slept until they called me to dinner…I went down stair…'

"Someone from the mob yelled out, 'Why did you say bloody spot?'

'I did say bloody spot. It's my way of speaking. My clothes have been sent to Cincinnati to be analyzed…I admit that I had blood on them…I have blood on me now from my nose…it is in the habit of bleeding and has bled since I started from town…I swear to you sincerely that I am innocent of that

230

crime. If you want to put me to death for that crime, I will have to die. But innocent blood will flow. I tell you the truth. I swear before God and man I'm innocent. Johnson and (Dan) induced the boys to say what they did. Innocent blood will flow if I have to die. As I said before, I'm innocent and know nothing whatever about it. I'm ready to die. Oh, God, comfort my poor mother and sisters and forgive you all. I'm innocent. I'm innocent of that crime.'

"It's exactly what I 'member him sayin', gist like Day recorded it. Yuh know, Tom, I think Teet shoulda been an actor or a politician. I remember how he sat again followin' his speech. He darn near took a bow. I commented under my breath. 'I remember Thornton sayin', "Me thinks he doth protest too much."

"The peddler used the word 'innocent' eight times as if repeatin' it would force it to come true. The word was in his last sentence, gist like he said it would be. To me, Mcleod's maneuvers seemed a desparate plea, as well as an attempt to blame the rest of us for the state he was in. He used his nosebleed. He made multiple references to his mother, and now included his sisters. He'd never spoke of havin' any sisters. Maybe mostly women was in the house. Maybe it's was why he was havin' so much trouble, huh, Tom?"

Tom rolled his eyes.

231

"I don't mean to taunt females. Mcleod probably gist concocted a few more women special fer the occasion, thinkin' they'd draw pity. I told the man standin' next to me, 'Maybe he thinks concerns fer a helpless female is what brought this group here, and he hopes girly references will raise enough sympathy to take down his noose. Come to think about it, Tom, up until John Brown and the Civil War, hangin' was considered a woman's way to die.

"He talked about 'breaking his mother's heart.' Maybe it's what he wanted all along, to break her heart like she broke his, and to git even fer his own pain, he broke Mary's and broke John and Sarah Sitterley's, and Grandpa Strouse's, and Fred and Kate's, and the whole community's.

"I can't believe I'm even sayin' this, but I did hear sometimes people who commit horrible murders have no memory of the event. If I woulda been Mcleod's lawyer, the only defense I coulda conjured up fer his 'I'm innocent' speech was 'maybe Mcleod completely blocked the dreadful deed out of his unhinged mind.'

"Yet, I have this gut feelin' everythin' Teet did was fer Teet. He'd planned each word of his last speech fer what he considered to be gist the right effect. He never could admit to bein' wrong. Mcleod used his 'poor me, I'm the victim here' ploy. He tried both of these: 'You will be the guilty ones, cause I'm innocent—then it will be your fault,' and 'it's Dan and Johnson's fault cause they induced the boys to say what they said.' His spiel went on and on. Of course, it would never be his fault!

"I said to the man standin' next to our wagon, 'I wouldn't trust Teet any further 'n I could throw him.' I didn't care if the peddler heard every word.

"Then I remembered my predictability list and decided, 'Guess the sheriff's right. I prob'bly could give Mcleod a better ratin'. Maybe he should be moved up with the others since his comments about bein' 'innocent' always gits connected to his mysterious mother. If I change his rank, everyone except Abs will be in a tie fer second place gist like Thornton recommended. Guess it's what happens when so many can't handle the truth. All the liars land in the same spot.

"The leader asked Abs and Jake fer their final words. In what had become familiar form, Abs admitted, 'Mcleod, Jake, and I did the rape. Mcleod did the murder.'

"I didn't read Ab's final statement to you, Tom. It's nearly identical with his midnight confession. You're prob-ly hankerin' to git home to do them dishes fer yer wife.

"Abs remained the winner on my predictability list. Who knows whether he understood the fate about to befall him.

Sometimes I found myself wishin' I could see into everyone's mind."

Duck Legs removed his scratched spectacles with the tarnished gold rims and sighed. "Absalom told me back at the jail how he'd always heard, 'Speak the truth and the truth will set you free.' It had set George free. It had set Jake free. It was the one thing Abs was good at. He, fer sure, wasn't smart enough to construct a good lie. Even when he would try, he'd follow it with the truth, but the truth never did set him free of anythin' other'n this wrinkly world."

"Jake's turn come next. What Jake said amounted to this: 'I am not guilty of murdering the girl. Mcleod told me he, himself, and Absalom had done the work.' Jake was short on words, like usual.

"I've always wondered why Jake now included Abs in 'doing the work,' instead of sayin', like he did at the hearin', 'Absalom was coerced by Mcleod.' I'm guessin' it was because Jake now felt the need to get even. Ab's midnight confession had landed the tall one back in the slammer and, only half a day later, in front of a lynch rope. He was sleep-deprived and hadn't had enough time to recover.

"Jake used only two sentences compared with Mcleod's seventeen. People pleasers usually don't have a lot of expressions of their own. I guess Jake gist had to learn the hard way how hangin' onto other's heels kin also mean hangin' onto their hells, and, in his case, could lead to gist plain hangin'.

"I told the man standin' by the wagon, 'Abs deserves a monument fer always tellin' the truth.' It was when I said the word 'monument,' it hit me like a bolt of lightnin'. I remembered King David's son, also named Absalom, had a monument built for himself.

"Though the king's son was smart and good lookin' and our Abs was neither, and though the king's boy rebelled against his father, and our Abs obeyed his pa, them Absaloms had something in common. It stirred me to the bone when I first thought of it."

"The man beside my wagon said, 'Yah, Deputy. I remember. The king's Absalom hung from a tree, too, a terebinth tree.

"Makes me wonder, 'what's in a name?' I'd never have put the spooky connection together if I hadn't said, 'Abs deserves a monument'."

Tom saw a tear fall down Deputy D.L.'s cheek.

Noticing Tom was watching, Deputy D. L. quickly wiped it away.

"Mcleod would have been the one who demanded the monument. He'd have wanted his name in giant letters, and he'd have wanted 'I'm innocent' inscribed below it."

"Right after our discussion, the wagon I was drivin' shook with a powerful jolt. I was sure Mcleod had gotten loose and was about to take me hostage. I angled to avoid the attack when I saw behind me, not Mcleod, but Elias, Mary's older brother.

"I questioned, 'What the heck? Are you thinkin' you can strangle the three of 'em yourself?'

"Elias ignored me. Instead he confronted the executioners, sayin', 'Stop! I don't think there's enough evidence'!"

"I said to the man next to the wagon, 'Oh, no, he believes Mcleod! The nose bleed musta convinced him.'

"Elias shouted to the crowd, 'I am an older brother of the murdered girl. I'm asking all of you to let one of the prisoners free, because I believe there is "reasonable doubt." Take him back to the jail. Give him a fair trial. I say this because more than one version exists about whether or not he was actually present when Mary was bludgeoned, and there's nothing to show Jake was around when her throat was slit.'

"It took me awhile to start breathin' normal again as the situation registered in my mind. 'Jake, not Mcleod.' I said it out loud a couple of times to convince myself. I wished Elias would add Abs to his request, but he didn't.

"The crowd watched as Mary's brother closed his eyes. Some thought he was prayin' or perhaps tryin' not to cry. Elias told me later, he was reconstructin' a scene from several years back when Mary's twin, Marion, had been sobbing under the old red oak tree in Grandpa Strouse's yard.

"I remember seein' Elias put his hand in his pocket and finger something. He said later, 'I touched my gold piece. Marion found it for me by the straw pile the same day I'd blamed him for stealing it and brought him to tears. The truth was, I had a hole in my pocket, and it had fallen out. Grandpa Strouse had given it to me. It was all I had to help me get started after my mother passed, and Calvin and I moved away to fend for ourselves. I've worked hard, so I never had to spend it. I've always been sorry I accused Marion falsely.'

"Since it was Mary's brother makin' the request, 'most everyone in the crowd agreed.

"Jake was stunned. He'd been set free twice in four days. This time he'd go back to jail for a third time, but he might not die. When they took down his rope, he wept.

"While most of the township and a lot of the county watched the lynchin', Sarah Sitterley sat at her kitchen table starin' at the note she'd writ to Mary. It was still visible on

Mary's slate. Though now smudged and blotched with Sarah's tears, she could still clearly read, 'There's no vinegar.'

"Sarah contemplated the comments she'd overheard about the prospective lynchin'. Somethin' John said about the event musta struck a nerve. She rose from the chair where she'd spent most of the past two weeks.

"She moved in the most decisive way she had since knowin' Mary was missin' and headed to the cupboard where she stored the tin. She retrieved all the pieces purchased from the peddler. She went out the back door to commence her own private execution. She was alone. John had gone to the lynchin'. John, who'd always been known fer teasin' and jokin', wasn't teasin', wasn't jokin', wasn't John, and Sarah wasn't Sarah."

"She procured the heavy ax from the woodpile. She could swing it pretty hard since she often used it to split small pieces fer their kitchen stove. Sometimes she'd used it to chop the heads off the chickens when they needed one to eat. But July eighth wasn't about splittin' wood or needin' a chicken to fry.

"Sarah carefully placed the metal pieces on a stone block. In a rush of energy, she swung her ax. The clatters and clangs rang through the humidity. The moisture acted like a megaphone. Her pain echoed off the walls of the barn. The thickness in the air did justice to her pent-up screams, creatin' a cussive display of rage. Shards of the cheap tin flew with every strike.

"When the pans and cups was cut and mangled to an unrecognizable state, Sarah stopped.

"She was out of breath. She told later how she'd gasped, 'You can split tin, but you can't split sin. Sin splits you.'

"Other'n her two-word testimony at the hearin', Sarah had said 'most nothin' since the dreadful, morbid Monday. She'd not heard her own voice.

"Sarah entered the house, pulled her hair back into a bun, and donned her apron. Reachin' across the dry sink, she touched the lye soap. Though cracked on top, the bar looked pure and clean. She knew what had been done with the soap. She gently touched it.

"Sarah told how she whispered to herself, 'I'm so glad,' then she hesitated, took a deep breath, and added, 'for this soap.' The scent activated in the water, smellin' like my room does now. Takin' still another deep breath, she warshed her dishes."

"Sarah did not wind the clock. Outside, she could hear the cornstalk metronome soothin'ly swayin' in the breeze, 'hush…hush…hush.' Them cornstalks was her time piece now."

239

CHAPTER 44 — FRED FACES THE COYOTE

Weeds grow in my garden, persistent soil graspers of the worst kind.

"Back at the lynchin', Fred watched the preliminary preparations. Of particular interest to him had been seein' two of his neighbors grab the opposin' handles of a cross-cut saw and work through a limb to support the suspension beam. The arm muscles Fred so often used fer the same process flexed as if they, too, was involved in this familiar motion. A smell of fresh sawdust slithered from the shavin's."

"Fred figured if they would have allowed the law to have its way, Mcleod or Absalom, or both, would eventually have faced a firin' squad, or a rope, or would, as others had suggested, be freed on some technicality. He saw the last prospect as 'unreasonable, reasonable doubt.'

"It seemed to Fred, time was a cheap commodity fer the legal community. A lot of it could be spent 'cause apparently they had a lot to spend. But to the farmer, time was precious. Farmers didn't have the summer to donate. They certainly couldn't travel to Ft. Wayne for a trial.

"Fred's mind fermented in the way of the ship's sauerkraut. Like Kate, with her mountain of laundry, he just wanted to end this nauseatin' struggle, and git on with the life he'd planned. He needed to deposit a farm payment. He desperately wanted a safe place fer his family and for their community. He wanted to sleep sound again, and he wanted to quit standin' cause his ankle hurt. He couldn't live like this anymore. He'd completely forgotten about 'haste makes waste.'

"Fred recalled reading in The Declaration of Independence: 'But when a long train of abuses and usurpations...evinces a design to reduce them under absolute Despotism, it is their right, it is their duty, to throw off such Government, and to provide new Guards for their future security...'

"*Do the right thing*, he thought. It didn't matter the season or the circumstance, a strong sense of responsibility always cloaked Fred, but on July the eighth, it darn near choked him. When you're a farmer, it's not right not to harvest in the season of harvest. Helping others, responsibility, and security was always in Fred's focus.

"Fred considered Mcleod's last words. The ribbon on the peddler's bridle, the blood on his knife, clothin,' and boot, and the lack of blood on his handkerchief spoke a different language than Mcleod's drawn-out "I have nosebleeds/I'm innocent" speech. Fred pondered, *What kind of man will lie in the face of death?*

"Then Fred recalled watchin' a k'eye-oat set up a deceitful scene one winter mornin' in the snow-covered field right next to their log cabin. A wild animal brave enough to venture so close to humans either had to be sick, rabid, or nearin' starvation.

"Apparently, the critter was tryin' to lure Fred's little dog, or maybe wanted to capture their small children who was out playin' in the snow.

"What struck Fred the most was how the animal yawned and stretched, so innocent-like. It lay down, appeared peaceful and tame, but its location and legacy registered inconsistent with its harmless display. The k'eye-oat was riskin' its life in a ruse fer survival.

"What Fred witnessed comin from the mouth of Mcleod seemed strikin'ly similar. Fred wondered what number of the crowd might get fooled by the huckster's last words. Fred considered the peddler's 'I'm innocent' speech to be the same as the k-eye-oat's yawn and stretch.

"Back at the jail, everyone remained bound. They attempted to free themselves and each other, but to no avail. Finally, Thornton said, 'Deputy D. L. will be back eventually. We might as well wiggle into the most comfortable positions we can and get some rest. Last night was one short night. Today might be one long day.'

"The sheriff guessed right concernin' his prisoners. He knew how farmers thought. He was learnin' how lawyers and judges operated. The handbook wasn't the same. Farmers didn't understand usin' all them words expended by the legal community to complicate the discussion before arrivin' at an obvious decision. Thornton reasoned, 'A farmer doesn't wait for weeks when he's found a chicken missing and a hawk is nearby with blood on its feathers.'

"He determined he'd arrest no one from the farmer mob. He told Dan, 'If anyone asks, I'll just say the jail couldn't hold them all, and not one of them offered me his name'."

CHAPTER 45 – THE CALL FOR VOLUNTEERS

Everything with feathers departed.

"When we first arrived, the birds in the woods was noisy. Then, all of a sudden, yuh coulda heard a leaf drop, 'cause everythin' with feathers disappeared.

"The workers adjusted the nooses. Absalom leaned forward fer 'em to place the rope over his head. His oily hair helped it slide right down. Mcleod moved his noggin from side to side, resistin' the rope.

"I can still see them two young men with the yellow and the reddish hair against that leafy green backdrop. The leader of the lynch mob who'd asked for their final words called fer those from Indiana who said they'd 'do the work.'

"No one stepped forward. I noticed Fred had his feet pointed away from the lynchin' like he was about to leave.

"The leader issued the call again. This time he was louder with his eyebrows drawn together. The whites of his eyes showed. He yelled, 'We're ready now for our volunteers!'

"No one came.

"The leader paused fer what seemed like ten country miles. This was the second thwartin' of the farmers' plans.

"Finally, the leader spoke in a blunt tone. 'Since no one from Indiana is courageous enough to answer the call like they said they would, I'll take five volunteers from Ohio.' His nostrils flared, his brows furrowed. He stared at the crowd, like he was huntin' the Hoosiers and might add ropes fer them, too.

"I saw Fred's foot turn back in the direction of the man in charge. Fred remembered thinkin', *This is starting to move like the hearing. If someone from Ohio steps forward, he'll probably be arrested later and might be hung for the murder of the murderers. Anyone who's smart, won't.*

"Again the call went forth as the leader's brow plowed another furrow. 'Perhaps you didn't hear me. We need five men. We've come this far. We can't go back now!'

"Fred's ankle throbbed. His stomach growled. His tongue and lips were dry. The slice of beef jerky was long gone, and his canteen had been drained. He felt delirious.

"He looked at Mcleod. Instead of a person, he was sure he saw a k'eye-oat."

CHAPTER 46 – BITE AND BE BITTEN

We are day transitioning into night.

Tom hadn't counted how many buckets he'd gone through, or how many times he'd refilled the pitcher on Phil's table. It seemed Deputy D.L. was drinking more as he recalled what happened at the lynching.

Phil leaned his body in toward Tom and said, "No one saw it comin'. Fred stepped forward. Four others joined him. The whites of their eyes showed above their pupils.

"The leader shouted, "pull!" At the same second, he motioned fer me to move the team forward. Minus the thirteen turns, the slip knots worked gist as well.

"Fred looked down. The last time he'd used a rope to exert this kind of force, he, with the help of John Sitterley and others, was stackin' the logs fer their cabin and raisin' their barn. Fred recalled his best friend's words on the witness stand.

He could hear the shards of anger in John's voice about how close Mary's murder was to Henry's.

"Fer a moment Fred felt exhilaration, like he wore the boots of a hero. He was doin' more than John's chores. Pickin' up the rope revived his hope to save his family, crops and community. It felt like he was helpin' John and Sarah git the retribution they deserved. But feeling 'high as a kite' didn't last any longer than some flirtatious July breeze.

"I remember clearly how the jury of what the papers said amounted to several thousand got silent, gist like them birds. Other than the Hoosier crows, no humans flew away.

"Fred told later the words 'one law...love your neighbor as yourself...' slid through his head. When them words got followed by 'Thou shalt not kill,' it was too late. I'd clucked to the horses. The wagon had shot forward. Fred had gripped to counter gravity. One at a time, both necks had snapped.

"Fred said he could feel the rough braids of sisal rope scrape his calloused hands. The coarse fibers sanded deep burns into the center of each of his palms. Yet, he and the four others kept the pull goin'. Fred's feet and legs pushed hard into the ground, leavin' bigger dents than his grindstone. His arm muscles ached. He grunted instructions to the others to alternate breaks. Each would take a turn in the order of their stance signalin' their need by sayin' the word 'rest.' Even with farmer muscles, it took a good ten minutes to hear the prisoners' last gasps as their final breaths left their bodies.

"To Fred's dismay, the leader said 'Leave 'em hang longer. We must be certain they're dead.'

"Though Fred didn't look at the victims, he could tell when their bodies turned 'cause the ropes rotated new blisters as well as burns onto his hands. The cross-beam squeaked, replacin' the bird squawks, as it drooped under the dead weight of the two young men. With each sound, Fred questioned if the limb was thick enough to withstand both hangin's.

"The air smelled like a latrine by the time their faces and fingernails turned blue while fifty other fingers and five other faces flushed bright red. I tried to hold my breath so as not to smell the body functions Mcleod and Abs could not control.

"Neither Fred nor I ever looked at their faces, though some said they did.

"Fred recalled how the lynchin' of John Brown had begun the Civil War. He'd read comments by Ralph Waldo Emerson who said, 'John Brown made the gallows glorious like the cross.' Brown had also said, 'Men cannot hang the soul.'

"As he became more and more weary, Fred began to second guess the process, *Was the right method chosen? Justice would have been better served if these men had been hung by another body part! I wish now I had brought my gun. Bullets would have been faster and made the job much easier, though we'd have desecrated Henry's soil with human blood, some of it his own.*

"Yuh know, Tom, in the end, death is death. Does the means really matter?"

Tom thought the means did matter. He'd seen enough slow, painful deaths at the infirmary to be sure of it, but he said nothing.

"George stood by the window checkin' his watch. I checked mine. At ten till four, after havin' pulled fer twenty minutes, the five with the red hands and faces was told they could let go.

"Fred noticed a button from his shirt amidst the weeds. Along with a blue fabric tatter, it had popped off when he started to pull. He put it in his pocket and leaned his shoulder against the mighty oak fer a few moments. I suspected he might pass out. His hair was in an unruly state. Then, without lookin' up, he limped away. He spoke to no one, not even his best friends. It wasn't like Fred to hang his head low. He mounted his horse from the wrong side cause of the pain in his ankle and headed home. Plenty of men remained to remove the corpses and the scaffold. Fred had done his part. He was known to be responsible. Now he was guilty of it.

"Someone offered the ropes to John Sitterley, but John declined. Knowin' pieces might get sold as souvenirs, John said, 'Burn the ropes.'

"Fred put his mare into the barn. He gave Sadie fresh water and grain. Even with the accumulation of horse manure, 'cause Fred hadn't had the time to remove it, Fred was sure his barn smelled better than either the courtroom or the lynchin'.

"When he entered their cabin, Kate gave him a concerned look. He removed his sweaty shirt and placed it along with the shell button on the table. He looked into Kate's pretty blue eyes and said, 'It is finished.' Takin' her hands, he kissed them. Then he turned over his rope-burned palms for her to see. She stared at him in disbelief.

"Fred put on his only other work shirt. Fresh off Kate's clothesline, it smelled like the life he longed to remember. He allowed himself a lengthy drink and splashed some water on his face. He washed his raw hands. Kate insisted on treating the rope burns on his palms. She went to the barn and brought in some horse liniment. She tore small strips of what remained of her wedding dress to wrap his wounds. She wondered if she'd have to sell the rest as rags to help pay for a lawyer when

Fred was arrested. She had hoped to keep the best piece, embroider a sampler, and have Fred frame it.

'You must eat.' Kate urged.

'I'm not hungry.'

'Then take this loaf of bread and some water with you.'

"As he limped to the field, Fred wondered when the officials would arrive. Though it was late afternoon, Fred determined to git everythin' done he could. He figured Kate's family would care fer her and their children. Though it would give her parents four extra mouths to feed, he knew his loved ones would be safe. Two of the predators was gone. The third would go to jail, at least for awhile until the circuit court came through again. *Jake and I might be cell mates.*

"Some Canadian thistles sprouted in his path. He referred to them as 'those old Canadee thistles.' He kicked 'em hard. Their prickly leaves flew high into the air. He never wanted any weeds from Mcleod's native land to grow on his property.

"Meanwhile, Kate procured a needle and thread. She repaired the fabric and sewed the button back onto a secure part of Fred's shirt. She quivered as she thought, '*A stitch in time saves nine' most of the time, but will it today?* When finished, she tossed the sweaty shirt into the basket. It was Fred's first item in next week's laundry. *Would it be his last?*

"Kate found herself cryin' as she prayed, 'Give us this day our daily bread...' Would Fred even be able to finish their harvest? She whisper-sang the words, hopin' to give the prayer more power.

"Unknowin'ly, out in the field, Fred joined in with the part about, 'Forgive us our debts as we forgive our debtors.' The words spurred his recall of Elias's plea, 'Don't kill Jake...' Tears drizzled clean paths down his dusty cheeks. The example of Mary's brother's ability to reach out to one of those accused was indeed remarkable.

"Fred had been sorrowful and afraid fer two weeks. Not fer himself, but fer the people and property he loved--Kate, his children, his community, his land and crops.

"Once the lynchin' was over, and Jake was bein' re-incarcerated, Fred released his old fears, but a new one grew in their place. It was as if God questioned him, *What have you done now?'*

"Fred worried, not only about losin' his loved ones, his crops, and his land, but about losin' his freedom. He knew he stood first in line fer punishment. He couldn't and wouldn't say 'I'm innocent.' He'd made the mistake of chosin' the wrong side of responsibility. His feelings shifted into guilt, shame, and regret.

He remembered, 'If you bite and devour one another, beware lest you be consumed.' Fred had joined the pack of humans determined to kill some predators. Now another powerful unit was undoubtably on its way to 'consume' him.

"He wondered, *Did I give up all I' slaved so many years for in one misdirected moment? I ignored the commandment 'Thou shalt not kill.' I even disregarded the meaning of my name. Frederick means 'peaceful ruler'.*"

CHAPTER 47 – THE LAW ARRIVES

A sleek angel glided her shiny spirit across a bumpy path.

"Let me say a little 'bout how lucky I was on the trip back with Jake. I took Tama Road all the way to the jail though a better route runs gist to the south. Of course, the officials chose the smoother way. Our paths never crossed, so I didn't have to answer one question about the lynchin'. And, lucky fer Sheriff Thornton, too, 'cause he didn't know anythin' 'bout what happened, other than he'd been broken into, bound, and his prisoners was gone.

"Also, I need to tell yuh, Jake did talk some after we returned to the jail. He told me how on the trip out, Mcleod mentioned havin' a wife...he called her 'the wife,' and never give her name. The tin peddler had told of a strange incident with her. The huckster had held his hands out, palms up, and instructed his wife to place hers on top of his. When she trustingly did so and relaxed, he jerked his away, causin' hers to fall. Then Mcleod laughed. It was same laugh Jake remembered hearin' when Mcleod raped Mary.

"I couldn't help but wonder if anyone had laughed when I pulled the wagon away leavin' Mcleod without support."

"Two hours later, around six p.m., gist as Fred expected, the men from the State of Ohio, includin' the Attorney General, and some said even the Lieutenant Governor, drove their fancy carriages with the shiny black wheels into Liberty Township. They turned onto dusty Tama Road. They'd probably never seen such a rutted path.

"The authorities came so far because they didn't want their state to acquire the awful reputation Indiana had fer mobs and lawlessness. Someone musta sent 'em a telegram for 'em to get to arrive as early as they did. I thought maybe it was the defense attorney, Callen. He was swingin' low from his losses, yuh know.

"Their intention was to arrest everyone involved in the construction of the gallows and the pullin' of the ropes. Havin' heard about the number of people who'd invaded the jail, and joined the group, they decided if they'd narrow it to these two, it would set an example and hopefully thwart any future lynchin's. They surmised they'd find traces of retribution at the site of Mary's murder even if the deed was done.

"To their great shock, not a twig was out of place. They never suspected it could have happened at Henry's.

"Fred heard 'em comin' before he saw 'em. Several units advanced in his direction. The first carriage was full. All the men toted guns, includin' the ones in suits. The second and third nearly empty units clearly awaited those they planned to capture.

"Fred didn't have a weapon, unless you counted his wooden farm fork. He readied his posture and reminded himself, I'm guilty. I have the fresh rope burns on my hands...obvious evidence. I'll only ask to bid farewell to Kate and the children. He remembered the broad ax in his dream...broken at the neck."

"Fred watched the units slow. The law looked directly at him. He stood next to a shock of wheat, fork posed to load it. The carriages stopped. Though some distance away, Fred could tell the officers had their guns pointed directly at him.

"A bee buzzed Fred's sweaty brow as the officials conversed. After what seemed like an eternity, one of 'em laid a line on the lead horse, and they all proceeded west. Fred waited fer 'em to turn around. He figured they'd decided, as a matter of efficiency, to pick up the neighbor at the end of the road first. They would get him on the way back when their units were pointed east toward the jail. Maybe they'd decided to wait until he left the field, so they didn't have to trounce through the wheat stubble to get him. Fred could have run and hid, but he didn't. He stayed in his field, and continued workin' with even greater haste than before though his ankle throbbed, and his palms burned with each lift of the fork.

"Meanwhile, Fred considered the murder he'd just committed. Killing was the reason his family had left Germany. He pondered havin' done somethin' so wrong coupled with what, at the moment, had seemed so right...destroyin' the 'k'eye-oats' to protect those he loved.

"He thought, *How will lynching Mcleod and Absalom ever reimburse John and Sarah, or Strouse's family, or this community for Mary's loss? Hanging those two didn't replace her. Nothing can. The only consolation we have now is those who acted like animals won't ever invade Tama Road again.*

An offer of remorse from Mcleod might have enabled John and Sarah to better cope, but Mcleod never once said, 'I'm sorry for your loss,' let alone admitted to her murder. Instead, the peddler begged for compassion regarding his mother's impending loss. He showed a lot of selfishness in the form of 'I only care what happens to me and mine.'

"Fred said it was at this point he caught a glimpse of his inkling to think the same. He remembered the thistles he'd kicked out on his way to the wheat field. He usually cultivated his fields early and often to keep the weeds down before they went to seed. Once the soil was well-tilled, Fred planted good seeds to crowd out the invaders and reduce the need for further tillin'. Fred thought, *Against good seed there is no law.*

"Fred's mind swirled as he attempted to process what he knew to be right, and to sort some great overridin' truth for humans from the unorderly pile of rules he'd acquired fer plants and animals. He'd chosen the principles he had for them...kill a k'eye-oat, kick out a weed. What was the same? What was different? Are humans unique? Do they require a separate set of rules, or perhaps, as the Bible and other religious readings indicate, a single rule, a Golden one?

"The thoughts agitated his mind like a grist mill, gratin' more severely than anythin' to which he'd subjected his corn or wheat. A rule fer survival seemed like a rule fer survival. In dealin' with plants and animals, execution woulda been the right thing. He'd destroy vile animals and weeds with no remorse, but in the human world, the answer was confusin'. Why and how were people different? Would, in fact, as the

259

preacher suggested, only 'the tame inherit the earth? What did it mean to be tame?'

"He heard the officials approach again, this time from the west. They didn't point their guns, or look at him, or even slow down. A horse whinnied as they faded from sight.

"To their angst, the attorney general and the others concluded they'd made a long dusty trip fer nothin'. They weren't able to find one smidgen of lawlessness in Liberty Township. Everything was peaceful. Men worked their fields. Women took down laundry, and children played in the yards. A girl walked alone on Tama Road.

"Their guns, their clothes, and their carriages were covered with more dust as they headed into town. There they also didn't locate one sign of a lynchin'…no scaffold, no ropes, no vigilantes with pistols, no bars full of people celebratin' the event, no pieces of rope for sale, no dead bodies awaitin' burial, and no freshly-dug graves. In case you're wonderin', Tom, two local doctors took the corpses fer medical studies as was the custom with criminals.

"For all the government knew, the mob had taken the suspects elsewhere, most likely across the state line into Indiana where Ohio lacked jurisdiction. The officials headed home. Indiana could deal with the crime.

"Nothin' to the contrary was known 'til weekly papers published the truth. The farmer mob had gotten away with murder. But unlike Mcleod, not one had attempted to run away. They'd hidden themselves in plain sight and left the state mighty embarrassed.

"Rather than risk further discredit, the State decided to turn the case over to the famous local prosecutor, F. C. LeBlond.

"Meanwhile, Fred made some sense out of his confusion by thinkin', Humans are like a coin with two sides…'heads,' 'love your neighbor,' is the tame side. 'Tails,' 'bite and be bitten in return,' is like animals, or like a small, untrained child, who's still teething and doesn't know any better than to bite to ease his pain.

"Fred wished he'd have favored the tame side. Fred wanted to 'inherit Erden.'

"Fred thought how Honest Abe, a log-cabin man himself, described the tame head of the coin as 'the better angels of our nature.' He wondered, *Could it be human beings are 'a little less than the angels' until they get scared or angry, and that's when the coin turns tails?*

"On July 8th, Fred farmed til the sun set in the west with not enough afterglow to outline a shock of wheat. No officers reappeared. Recognizin' he wouldn't be 'bitten in return,' Fred grabbed a handful of stalks. They covered his rope-burned palm.

"More tears than he had wheat fell down his soiled cheeks. He thought, *Soul building doesn't come any easier than soil building.*

"I forgot to tell yuh, Tom, Fred's first name was John. He didn't go by it 'cause of his namesake, Uncle Frederick, and also 'cause of John Sitterley livin' so close by. The meanin' of the name 'John' is 'God is gracious.'

"Fred returned to their cabin and ate a small portion of the dinner Kate had saved. He stopped to watch Emma sleep, and gently rocked the walnut cradle.

"Finally, Fred rested the best he had in two weeks, not 'cause of the death of the predators, but 'cause he'd begun the process of puttin' his fearful side to sleep. However, for many a month, when someone knocked on their door, Fred's eyes widened."

CHAPTER 48 — AUGUST, 1872

Milkweeds podded. Thistles sequenced from purple blossoms to dusty white blobs. Early locusts sang themselves free of their shells while nature cloud-painted her sky.

Tom still had a small area in the middle of Phil's floor to mop. He said, "Deputy, I need to move you, your chair, your table, and your bed."

With the furniture rearranged, the old man fiddled with his glasses trying to decide whether to leave them off or on. He left them off.

"I want to talk now about an event at Maggie's store. Maggie was busy with her inventory in the back room. She wondered what to do with the remainin' spools of No. 9 green ribbon. It was one of her more expensive types 'cause of bein' the widest she carried, and because it was finely ribbed. Only a few of her clientele could afford it.

"After Mary's murder, Maggie considered either everyone would want to buy a sample of the ribbon to honor Mary, or no one would be able to bear the sight of it, 'cause it reminded 'em of the tragedy. She found the latter to be true. No green ribbon had been sold since early June. She left one spool on the shelf in case a change of heart occurred.

"While Maggie pondered her dilemma, she heard the bell on her shop door jingle, signifyin' the entry of a customer. She peeked from behind her workroom curtain. On the counter, she noticed the much-avoided roll of green ribbon. The patron who'd placed it there now faced the front of the store. The woman's form was thin. She dressed in black. Maggie couldn't recall any shopper bearin' such a tiny silhouette though the wide-brimmed bonnet she wore looked strangely familiar.

"As Maggie crossed the creaky floor, the shopper turned to face her.

"Maggie exclaimed, 'Sarah Sitterley! I'm so glad to see you.'

"Maggie hadn't seen her since the trial. If anythin' was needed from the store, John came. Mrs. Sitterley looked like she'd lost nearly thirty pounds."

'How are you, Sarah?'

"Sarah breathed deeply, capturin' the scents of lavender and cinnamon before she spoke. 'I'm doing better...I've come to

264

purchase some green ribbon. I worried you might not have any.'

'I still have a supply. How much would you like?'

'A couple of yards should be enough.'

"Maggie unrolled the ribbon with extreme care. She said it seemed like she'd entered a sacred space. She found it difficult to cut but managed the task. She gently folded it, goin' back and forth in about eight-inch segments, placin' ribbon on top of ribbon 'til the remnant ended. She placed it on thin wrappin' paper and encased it. She sacked it in one of the pretty hand-made cloth bags she reserved fer fabrics.

"Sarah asked, 'What do I owe you?'

'There is no charge for the ribbon, Sarah. You've paid the price.'

'Thank you, Maggie. It's for Mary.'

"Maggie gasped.

"Sarah kept talkin' like she hadn't heard Maggie's response. 'The pink surprise lilies have bloomed. Some people call them resurrection lilies. I was so glad to see them this morning. I just had to have some of Mary's special green ribbon to tie around them. I plan to take them to her grave.'

"Maggie breathed a sigh of relief. Fer a moment she'd had the impression Sarah might have imagined Mary to still be alive, or to have resurrected with the lilies. She'd heard sometimes grief will have strange effects on a person.

"Maggie said, 'I know you will create a lovely bouquet for Mary. Everything you bought and did for her was so beautiful.'

'Thank you. And thank you for the ribbon, Maggie. John and I are so grateful to have had Mary in our lives, even for such a short period. I guess you've heard our farm is for sale. After the corn is harvested, we're moving south to a place closer to the Ohio River and starting over. The new county is called Fairfield. I like the name.'

"Maggie came from behind the counter. She handed the cloth bag to Sarah and gave her a hug. Maggie said, 'We'll miss you Sarah, but we understand. Fairfield is a beautiful name.' Repeatin' Sarah's usual by-words, Maggie added, 'I'm so glad.'

"As she waved good-by, Sarah clutched the bag of green ribbon to her chest like a mighty poultice and murmured her newest catch-all phrase. 'It's just the way it is…' "

CHAPTER 49 — RETRIBUTION

The smells from the kitchen fluctuated like the clouds in the sky.

Tom had finished scrubbing all there was to scrub, including the window sill and doorknob. But it was obvious the deputy wasn't done. He put the scratched lenses back on his wrinkly face and carefully opened his diary.

'Bet yuh thought this story was over, Tom. Well, surprise to us all, it wasn't. And surprise to me, I got distracted with movin' furniture and Maggie's store and neglected to fill in the part about F. C. Leblond, the famous prosecutor the state asked to take legal action against those who'd done the lynchin'. Fred and the others was not off the hook.

"The Honorable Leblond was the oldest member of the bar in our county. An ex-congressman, he'd been born in the United States, gist like John Sitterley, the second generation in a time when many others was only first-generation immigrants. LeBlond's father had been sent over by his grandparents to avoid military service under Napoleon. LeBlond had been a prosecutin' attorney since 1847 when Fred was only seven years old. Havin' traveled around the legal block a time or ten, F. C. had earned a record fer doin' right. He'd established school laws and become famous for his help after the Civil War in the reconstruction of the union. He was smart and handsome, which don't hurt none, yuh know, when involved in law and politics. So, like I already mentioned, the lieutenant governor and attorney general put him in charge of prosecutin' those who did the lynchin'.

"Fred experienced more than a few sleepless nights wonderin' what the Honorable F. C. might do. Though he didn't know the man personally, he'd seen him bite at the hearin', and was aware of his near-perfect reputation...somethin' Fred knew he, himself, no longer had.

"To the astonishment of all, the prosecutor chose not to prosecute. The local newspapers supported his decision by never printin' the names of any of the men who were responsible, though one article had pointedly said, 'Prominent men were involved in the lynching.' A prosecutor can't prosecute if he don't have any names of who he should prosecute, huh, Tom?"

"Some two years later, in 1874, people had settled into routines as close to normal as possible on Tama Road. The Sitterley's had made the move to Fairfield County. Fred had helped John load their big wagon. The morning they were to leave, Fred got up early. He brought his broad ax out of the house with him. He carried his grindstone out of the barn and placed it on the four familiar dents in the ground. No rooster had crowed, and the chickens' heads were still tucked beneath their wings. When the tool was shiny sharp, and iron filings peppered the dirt, he returned his grindstone. He kissed the broad-ax and snuck across the road to the Sitterleys. He tucked the ax into an inconspicuous spot on their wagon. He wanted John to have it in case he had to build a cabin on their new property. *It was not broken at the neck.*

"Kate had packed what she hoped was enough food to hold 'em for the long trip. Fred left the basket of vittles on the wagon seat. As he was about to enter their cabin, he saw John and Sarah exit their beautiful home for the last time. Fred and Kate had already bid them farewell, but John pulled to a stop and waved for Fred to come.

'I saw you sneaking around my wagon this morning, like a thief, but I know you, Fred, and you were a thief in reverse.

Here's your broad-ax. Thank you so much, but I can't take one of your prize possessions, Fred. It should be passed down in your family as a way to remember how hard you worked for your land and all you sacrificed. I promise I'll remember how to cut the handle crooked, if I should need one, and I promise I'll never forget our friendship.'

"With tears in their eyes, they drove off into the sunrise. Though Fred and Kate missed them, Fred found he could farm without John after all. John made decisions without Fred, as well, though both still believed 'two heads are better than one' when it comes to plantin' and harvestin'.

"Fred trimmed his beard regularly again, and to the onlooker his crops appeared weedless. Phebe said her mama's cookin' 'tastus good', and once in awhile Kate sang somethin' other'n a lullaby. For each day with everyone safe, the community breathed a sigh of relief.

"Occasionally suspicions did surface about whether the right men had been lynched. Rumors were spread about a man from Blackcreek Township who'd slit his throat on the day of the lynchin.'—the grape vine said it was cause he thought the farmer mob had learned the truth and was headin' in his direction.

CHAPTER 50 — SNOW STORM

Identical ice-cycles dripped from tree limbs in near perfect order while small purple blossoms struggled through frozen white mounds, trying their best to find the sun.

"A late spring snowstorm postponed the farmers' plans to begin work in the fields.

Mcleod was gone, but the horror he'd left behind hadn't melted. It invaded most every layin' down and wakin' up. Though the citizens spoke of it less and less, and the surroundings and people took on the outward appearance of before June 23, 1872, the residents of Tama Road still relived the events daily. With each rising and settin' of the sun, it was the first thought to enter and the last to leave their minds. The impact was buried deeper than anythin' covered by a mound of snow.

"Confined to their homes by the inclement weather, most everyone in the county focused on their weekly newspaper. An article of interest appeared on March 26, 1874, exactly one day before Mary would have celebrated her fifteenth birthday. The paper had printed a telegram sent to the Commercial T. It told of a confession given to a priest by someone named Thomas Bradwell Douglas. It said the strange confession 'was recorded in Denver, Colorado, as Douglas lay on his deathbed.'

Deputy D.L. shuffled through some newspaper clippings, then began reading:

'In this my dying hour, in hope of full pardon, by confessing the deed that has weighed upon my mind like a death pall, I am the guilty wretch who outraged and murdered Miss (Mary Arabelle)...Heaven alone knows what hellish motive prompted it, but at the time my brain was on fire from drink. I was veritable a madman past power of control. The hanging of Mcleod and (Absalom) was murder. I was one of the mob that executed them. I hope God will pardon me: that the families of Mcleod and (Absalom) will be relieved of this stigma of dishonor. I have but a few moments to live, and with my last breath, I avow the truth of all my statements herewith.

Thomas B. Douglas

"Some of the surnames mentioned, which I'll not give, was misspelled in the telegram. A notice signed with the words 'by the priest who took the confession' was attached. The priest's name wasn't included.

"Sheriff Thornton awakened every morning to the image of Mary's desecrated body bloatin' in her grave. Upon readin' the article, Thornton raised his eyebrows and drew them together like when he was workin' a problem. He and I both questioned the words. He said, for him, it revived the sight of the dry blood on Mcleod's clothin', knife, and handkerchief...specks Thornton was certain hadn't flowed from the huckster's nose... evidence set for eternity on a blade and some cloth."

"Fred rocked increasin'ly slower as he read and reread the article. Though he was sittin' close to the fire, the words left him cold. He dropped the paper on his lap and viewed his scarred palms. Bein' too responsible had taken its toll. Fred had to learn there are items in this life a man can fix and put away, and items he can't. Soul buildin', fer sure, didn't come as easy as carpenterin', clearin' land, sharpenin' a broad ax or a scythe, or farmin'. It was a whole different form of cultivatin'.

"Fred worried, *Did I help lynch the wrong men?* He didn't think so, but the untimely confession jolted his composure.

Revertin' to his German accent, he thought to himself, *Two wrongs don't make a right. Too soon old, too late schmart.*

"Another 'bite' had appeared. The chain of fear added one more link continuin' the circle of fangs, tooth after tooth, link after vicious link.

"Fred worried extra black marks had been added to his name in the ever after. He remembered the stories of how St. Peter greeted people at the Golden Gate when they passed from this life into the next with a tally in his hands to determine if the person could enter. Fred had killed. If he'd hung innocent men, more lines would get added, in addition to the one fer snappin' at Kate about the burnt offerin's, as well as his recurrin' sins toward pride when he chopped the last visible weed or felled another acre of trees.

"Fred had come close to losin' everythin' on July eighth. If the officials had arrested him, he woulda had to pay the consequences. He wouldn't have blamed Kate, or the angry crowd, or a reptile. He wouldn't have given up his sense of responsibility. Never would he part with that.

"Fred thought most of his fears had exited with the shiny black carriages, and the rest had evaporated with F.C. LeBlond's decision, but for a third time, the same old boulder shadowed a nasty snake, and like the meltin' rows of ice cycles outside his cabin window, dripped a row of chillin' memories.

274

"Also reading on March 24, 1874 was Callen. Remember him, Tom? He'd been a defense attorney durin' the hearin'. Although he'd represented Mcleod, how could he believe in the huckster's innocence? All the evidence pointed to the peddler's guilt. Callen's only hope of winning had been to eliminate Henry's sons as credible witnesses. The prospect evaporated when George changed his story back to his original version. Callen's defense team, no matter how hard they tried, couldn't alter the bloody knife, spotted handkerchief, blood-stained clothin', or the girl's ribbon found tied to Mcleod's horse's bridle.

"By contrast, the Douglas article mentioned nothin' concrete except the man's name, a nameless priest, and the far-away city of Denver. No path of who he'd connected with in the community emerged to reconstruct anythin', a rare happenin' in a small rural community where people liked knowin' each other's business and remembered clearly anyone new who came or went.

"Callen said he'd investigate further. If he exonerated Mcleod now, it would probably help his law practice. Because he'd represented the peddler, people didn't much like him. Most still avoided givin' him their business.

"Even if he wasn't able to clear his clients, possibly he could git more favorable notice among the locals fer tryin' to find out the truth. For sure he'd get plenty of news coverage.

"After a time, Callen told the paper, 'No deaths were reported in Denver on January 12, 1874, the date the priest claimed to have given Douglas his last rights. In fact, no deaths in Denver preceded or followed the twelfth, let alone the death of someone named Thomas Bradwell Douglas.'

"Callen contacted all the priests in the Denver area. Not one remembered the Douglas confession. And an editor from The Denver Post claimed no such article had appeared in their newspaper. Nor could anyone by the name Thomas Bradwell Douglas be traced as havin' ever lived there.

"When finished, Callen published his discoveries in the local paper. As Fred read the update, he recognized his third batch of grace. This time no officials was involved. His own mind would have to pass the final judgment. The way to find peace was to forgive himself. And he knew, the only way to be totally free was to tell the truth.

"Kate scraped the bottom of her iron pot with a long-handled spoon. The metal grated as she removed the bits prone to stick and burn. Near the edge of the pot, the spoon suddenly stopped with a clunk. Kate scooped the obstruction onto a ladle and lifted it from the pan.

'It's interesting to see what's left in the soup when the broth and froth have boiled away. It's only then you can find the contents.'

"Kate moved the utensil, and with her hand underneath to catch any drips, carried it to Fred. Fred saw a gray, oil-coated blob.

"When Kate called the family to dinner, she placed the rock on a small plate in the center of their trestled table. Phebe and Anton eyed each other. Baby Emma giggled. Anton squirmed. Fred said his usual prayer, 'God is good and God is great, and we thank him for our fould. By His hands we all are fed. Give us Lord our daily bread. Amen.'

"Kate picked up the plate. She passed the stone to the two oldest children. Wide-eyed, Phebe handed it to Anton who was seated next to her. Neither touched it. Finally, Phebe spoke.

'I know who put the stone in the soup, but I'm not telling.'

"Fred said, 'Guess every family finds at least one rock in their soup now and then. No one seems to want to eat it though, or fess up about how it got there, do they, Anton?

"Anton lowered his head. 'I put it in the soup. Did I ruin it?'

'Thank you for being honest, Anton. It takes a real man to tell the truth. No, it didn't ruin the soup, but it might have dislodged someone's front tooth if they bit into it.'

"Fred paused. 'Kate, please bring the good food to the table. Because Anton told the truth, there'll be no punishment. We know you won't do it again, will you, Anton?'

"Anton agreed before his father had a chance to change his mind. He said, 'I promise, Papa. No more stone soup.'

"As Fred ate, he thought about what time might find in the broth once his life had boiled away. He considered how he'd taken the path of fear and tripped on a rock where the snake hid. Behaving like a predator, he'd bitten in return and nearly knocked more than a front tooth out of his life. He also thought a lot about what it takes to tame little boys and girls.

"He vowed when his children got older, he'd tell 'em about the tin peddler murder, and what he did because he was afraid. Perhaps they would learn from his mistake.

"Fred had had all he ever wanted of bitin' and the tail's side of the coin. He determined he'd focus on the 'love your neighbor' side and try his best to bring out what Lincoln referred to as 'the better angels of our nature.' Fred thought, By some mysterious intervention, we humans have the power to be more than an animal, but it looks like everyone must seek and find the path for him or herself.'

"Fred finished his soup. He left the table to work in the barn. As he departed, he winked at Kate, touched the pine trunk, and stopped to gently rock the walnut cradle. He recalled his dream about the broad ax. It had been broken *at the neck*. He had sought to have it welded.

"The early spring snow melted, but it was too wet to begin tillin' the fields. So, when Fred got to the barn, he picked up his grindstone and took it outside. He placed it in four familiar dents in the snow and went back in to get his scythe. He'd use this down time to ready himself for the eventual harvest. As he pedaled to speed up to gist the right whirrin' sound, he glanced over at Sitterley's. Their new neighbor was outside and lookin' toward him. Fred waved. The neighbor headed in his direction. After exchangin' greetings, the neighbor joked with Fred about being ready for a wheat crop three months early. Fred smiled. 'I can see green blades peeking through the snow. By the way, remind me how was it you came to settle in this neck of the woods'?"

CHAPTER 51 – GOOD THINGS GROW

Walk lightly on the earth and leave a blue sky.

Tom stood by the door, ready to leave. He determined, he'd help his wife do the dishes. But Phil still had more to say. Tom leaned against the door jam to listen.

"Yuh know now it was a big story that happened in a little place. Given time good can grow even in the manure of a predator. People can be tamed enough to at least be civil. Let me tell yuh how it was...

"Jake remained in jail fer a little more than four months until he was processed in the Court of Common Pleas. Get this, Tom. They released him on November the thirteenth. Good fer Jake, it weren't on no Friday. Fer him, I'm guessin' it was like unwindin' the unlucky number of turns in a lynch rope." Phil glanced at his diary and said, "Pushin' five months in the slammer, Jake's jail fees amounted to around eighty dollars and twenty-five cents. If my memory serves me, it would have been enough to buy a small farm back then.

"As for Thornton, on the lengthy trip to Ft. Wayne to arrest our suspects, he recognized the value of travelin' on planks instead of muddy ruts. Once he finished his four years as sheriff, he and his sons launched a construction business. They improved many area roads and built a race track at the same fairgrounds where the farmer mob hatched its strategy to steal our prisoners.

"Strouse buried his wife a little more than a month after Mary died. Matchin' headstones mark their graves. Mary has a rose on hers. 'Guess no one wanted the lily to lose more petals. I heard, only a few years later Grandpa Strouse got thrown from a buggy when his horse acted up. People said he died instantly of, of all things, a broken neck.

"Fred spent the rest of his life doin' what he loved best. He outlived Kate. They had a lot of practice taming babies, ten who lived. He served his family and community, and even got elected to some public offices.

"But Jake weren't the only one invaded by the number thirteen. Fred and the farmer mob got hit hard in 1875 by the worst floodin' we'd ever seen. It held the record fer rain in our parts amountin' to, get this, Tom, some recorded thirteen inches durin' the month of July alone. Fred couldn't help but think of the number of turns on the regularly constructed lynch rope. Perhaps the Creator made His ropes out of water, and the farmer mob was bein' 'consumed fer bitin' gist like it said in Galatians.

"The 'cessive rain began in the spring, but July was the worst. Fred prayed fer help and forgiveness. Because the downpours started early, he was smart enough to construct raised beds fer his crops, like they did back in Germany. His extra efforts paid off. Water filled the ditches instead of the rows. Though his corn fired at the base and yellowed at the top, he still reaped enough of a harvest for their farm payment.

"He and Kate had more children...first a son in 1873 who I'm sure you'll be surprised to know they named John. They named the next child William. He was born in 1875 when it flooded. In 1877, they had a little girl and named her Mary, in honor of both Mary 'Belle and Kate's mother. Her middle name was Catherine, Kathrina in German, after Kate. She was pretty, with a round face gist like her mama's. But Mary Catherine died at four or five weeks. Fred made a tiny oak casket. He trimmed it in walnut. They buried her in the Kessler Cemetery. Her tombstone has a little bird at the top, exactly like the one on Mary's locket. Fred wondered if her death was yet another example of being 'consumed.'

"Nearly a decade later, Fred and Kate found a sign of grace in the walnut cradle. On *July 8th*, 1886, not thirteen, but a lucky fourteen years to the day after the lynchin', Kate gave birth to their tenth child, a son they named Lewis.

"When old enough, Fred made sure the boy knew what had happened on the day of his birth back in 1872.

"To show his gratitude, Fred built Kate a beautiful new house. It had an ice box—saw it myself. When it was finished, they carried Baby Lewis over from their log cabin in the walnut cradle. Eventually, Lewis inherited the trunk that came from Germany and the broad ax, but he'd have to build his own cradle.

"Fred focused the rest of his life on plantin' only good seeds. I do need to tell yuh, though, about one more remarkable dream, might have been a part of the legend, but here it is: Fred dreamed about his trip over on the packet ship. The ocean waves tossed and turned. People swayed from side to side. Durin' the storm, Fred got lost from his parents. He could see himself from the back, wanderin' around on the ship's deck, wearin' the small hat he remembered ownin', hangin' onto it with both hands to keep from losin' it in the wind. He pushed through the crowd, desperate to find his folks. But when the small boy wearin' the hat turned his face, low and behold, it wasn't him after all. The lost little boy was Alexander Mcleod.

283

"Ten years prior to Fred's passin', what I'm gonna read next was printed about him in the county history book."

Phil adjusted his glasses for his last reading. He found the page:

'(Fred) was educated in both German and English in the schools, and since leaving school has by private reading and study acquired a large fund of general information, which is very useful to him in his life work, and which he has always been willing to use for the benefit of his fellow-men...Now he owns in all 200 acres of fine land, and has of this nearly 120 acres under cultivation...In all areas of farming, he has been unusually successful...He is public spirited, using only judicial prudence in connection with lending aid to enterprises bidding for public support, and being always ready and willing to aid such as offer a reasonable prospect of benefiting the community at large. All recognize in (him) a man of thorough trustworthiness, the head of a respectable family, true to every relation in life, religious, social, and moral, as well as one of the wealthiest and most successful farmers of his township."

Phil added, "I've wondered often if the severe tests of evil don't git given to some of us, maybe all of us, to see if we kin work our way out of the reptile's dust, and the fear, and back to the side of love.

"Fred did add one more sayin' to his collection, not about bitin' but about the tame side of the coin. He'd often say, 'You can catch more flies with honey than with vinegar.'

"The last time I stopped by to see him, he got new spectacles. Like me, he only ever used 'em fer readin'. I could tell he was ailin' some. I asked him about his health. He laughed, patted his tummy, which had expanded quite a bit through the years 'cause of Kate's good cookin', and said, "I'm on the level, Phil. My bubble's in the middle."

"As far as I could find, no one ever discovered who sent the Thomas Bradwell Douglas telegram, though I have my suspicions. Only a few mighta profited. Another bit hit a paper in 1926, givin' what I think was a clue. We's out of time today though, Tom. If you're interested, we kin follow through later.

"As fer me, when Thornton's four-year term was up, I switched jobs, too. Get ready to be shocked, cause I had to add my own name to my predictability list, and I put it on the bottom line right next to Teet's. I'd become completely unpredictable.

Phil removed his glasses and placed them reverently on his bedside table. He spun them a few times, chuckled, and pulled out his suspenders for his big announcement:

"I became a peddler!

"Close your mouth, Tom, or you'll swallow the fly that's been pesterin' us. The only predictable part was I didn't sell tin. No tin peddlers would ever be welcome on Tama Road again. Instead I sold spectacles, same as the ones I wear now. I always wanted to see into people's minds. I wanted others to see better, too.

"I never married. I worked as a salesman 'til I come here to the Infirmary. I was in my twenties when this all started. I'm over eighty now, yuh know.

"Back to finishin' the part about good growin' out of manure…What restored Fred and Kate's spirits after Belle's murder, the year of the terrible floodin', and the loss of Mary Catherine, was a postcard from John and Sarah Sitterley. It come by rail, all the way from Fairfield County, some seven years after the tragedy. Kate let me copy the words when I stopped by on my annual peddlin' trip, cause by then she had to wear spectacles full time. They'd gist got it when she showed it to me. She asked me to pass the good news on when I made my stops.

"It read:

'Dear Fred and Kate,

'We're so glad to let you know we are the proud parents of a baby boy. Following you, we chose to name him William, or "Willahelm" in German. As you know, it means "will for a helmet" or "desire for protection." We hope to bring our little Will back home to meet yours when he's old enough to travel. We'll visit both of our Marys' graves. We'll let you know when we're coming.'

'Your friends forever,

John and Sarah Sitterley.'

"Though good finally come from the manure, I'm sorry to add, as yuh well know, mankind still isn't tame. It's one thing to say it's 'cause we're a snarlin' animal, and another to say it's 'cause we're afraid. I think all them snarls comes from the fears. Sometimes it's fears we're not good enough, and sometimes it's the fear of havin' to be the responsible ones 'cause we really might be, as Lincoln said, 'a little less than the angels.' Strange as it is, we've got these thoughts of bein' both victims and heroes. And them fears of not gittin' what we lust after has done us in, all the way from the apple on…

"At any rate, it was the way it was, Tom, a big story, in a small place, with lots not fittin' the grounds of civility. There was too much blood and a whole river of tears. Fer better or worse, it was over. No one spoke of it much, 'cept maybe around their kerosene lamps at night, and sometimes, once a year, near the time fer the farmer's picnic, where it slowly become the stuff of legend, like an aged quilt, still useful, though frayed about the edges."

As Phil spoke, he reached over to touch his comforter. In the center was a tie made from an old green ribbon.

Outside the Golden Meadows Home, through the sparkling open window, the cornstalk metronome whispered, "hush. . . hush. . . hush."

Bibliography

[?]. Retrieved July 26, 2013, from Fairfield County Oh
    Archives Photo Tombstone. . . . Sitterley, John and
    Sarah:http://files.usgwarchives.net/oh/fairfield/photos/
    tombstones/lithopolis/Sitterley422nph.txt

[?]. (1872, July 4, 11, 18; November14). Articles from the
    Celina Journal. *Celina Journal.*

[?]. (1872, June 27; July 18; August 8; November 14). Articles
    related to the murder of Mary Secaur. *Mercer County
    Standard*, p. [?].

[?]. (1872, July 9, 10). "The Lynching in Mercer County."
    Cincinnati Gazette.

[?]. (1872, June 28; July5). "A Little Girl   Murdered...;
    Murder"*Van Wert Bulletin.* (6/28/1872;7/5/1872;).

[?]. *A Portrait and Biographical Record of Mercer and Van
    Wert Counties*, Ohio. (1896).

[?] "A Terrible Affair." (1872). *Indiana Herald,* Huntington,
    IN (July 3, 1872).

The Holy Bible--King James Version. Cleveland, Ohio. World.

[?]. "The Secore Murder, A Fearful Sequel." (1872, July 10).
    Indiana Herald (July 10, 1872).

Adams County Poor Farm. (2014, November 12). Retrieved
    November 17, 2015, from Adams County Poor Farm -
    AsylumProjects:

http://www.asylumprojects.org/index.php?title=Adams
_County_Poor_Farm. . . .

Bailey, C. (1867). Allen County Gazeteer Directory of Ft.
Wayne. Chicago, Illinois: C.W. Bailey.

Becker, Ernest. (1975). Escape From Evil. New York: The
Free Press. (p. 169).

Bennett, Karen. Various emails. 2018.

Briggs, Andrew. (2016-2018). J.H. Day research. (Sharon
Cowen, Interviewer).

Brice. (1868). The History of Ft. Wayne. Ft. Wayne,
Indiana: D.W. Jones.

Bushell, S. M. (2007). Historic Photos of Ft. Wayne.
Nashville, Tennessee : Turner Publishing Co.

Campbell, J. (1988, June 1). The Hero's Adventure. The
Power of Myth. Bill Moyers. PBS.

Census.(1870, 1880). United States Government. Heritage
Quest: http://www.censusrecords.com

Child   Found   Dead.   (1872).   Mercer   County
Standard(6/27/1872).

Covenanter.org. (?). Alexander Mcleod. Retrieved August
16, 2013, from Biographical Sketch of Alexander Mcleod
(1772-1833):

http://www.covenanter.org/McLeod/alexandermcleod.htm

Day, J. H. *Lynched! A Fiendish Outrage--A Terrible Retribution.* Celina: Mercer County Standard. (1872).

Employee, E. (public access/public domain). File:EM-spectrum. png-Wikipedia, the free encyclopedia. Retrieved November 11, 2013, from File:EM-spectrum.png: http://en.wikepedia.org/wiki/File:EM-spectrum.png

www.find-a-grave.com. (various).

Frech, H. (2014, July 11). Questions regarding The Tin Peddler Murder of Mary Secaur. (S. Cowen, Interviewer).

Hassett, K. "The County Home in Indiana: A Forgotten Response to Poverty and Disability." (2013, May). Retrieved August 4, 2013, from http://cardinalscholar.bsu.edu/:www.poorhousestory. com/poorhouses_in_indiana.htm

Heritage Quest. (n.d.). HeritageQuest Online - Census Image. RetrievedAugust28,2013,fromheritagequestonline.com: http://persi.heritagequestonline.com/hqoweb/library/do/census/result...

Hoehn, E. N. (2007). *Human Anatomy and Physiology.* San Francisco: Pearson Benjamin Cummings.

Jenkins, G.W., Kemnitz C P. , & Tortora, G. J. (2007). *Anatomy and Physiology, from Science to Life.* Hoboken, NJ,: Wiley.

Karen's Chatt. (2018). karen@karenmillerbennett.com.

Kimmel, David. (2011-2018) Various emails and conversation regarding Tin Peddler Murder.

Lamott, A. (2013). *Stitches: A Handbook on Meaning, Hope and Repair*. New York: Riverhead Books.

Loomis, E. A. (1960). *The Self in Pilgrimage*. New York: Harper and Brothers.

Luming, C. C. (2010, January 9). "Terebinth Tree." Retrieved August 3, 2013, from "The road less traveled...: TerebinthTree:"http://jigsawpuzzleoflife.blogspot.com/2010/01/terebinth-tree.html

McMurray, W. J. (1923). *History of St. Marys, Auglaize County, Ohio* (Part 1). (Historical Publishing Company) Retrieved June 26, 2014, from http://history.rays-place.com/oh/aug-st-marys-1.htm

Mercer County Jail Register, 1872. (1872).

Mercer County Ohio Railroad Stations. (?). Retrieved September 15, 2015, from www.west2k.com/ohstations/mercer.shtml

Midlam, T. (2003). "Mercer County Ohio." Retrieved August 6, 2013, from DCOWEB: http://mercer.dcoweb.org/

Midlam, T. (2003). "Mercer County Liberty Township." Retrieved August 6, 2013, from Mercer County Ohio: http://mercer.dcoweb.org/liberty1.htm

Minnich, Lucas. (2017). Various emails and Parkway High School class walk down Tama Road.

North Jersey Media Group. (?2013). 'Touched by an Angel' creator returns with Hallmark movie, "Signed, Sealed and Delivered". Retrieved November 11, 2013, from NorthJersey.com:http://www.northjersey.com/arts_ente rtainment/television/22733956

Obituary: Kromer. (1936). *Ft. Wayne Journal Gazette* (July 31, 1936). Ft. Wayne, Indiana.

Pryer, T. (1872). Mary Secaur's Death. Journal of I. F. Raudabaugh, [?].

Riso, Don Richard. *Personality Types--Using the Enneagram for Self-Discovery.* (1996). New York: Houghton Mifflin Harcourt.

Sanford, J. A. (1968). *Dreams: God's Forgotten Language.* NewYork: Harper Row.

Schaadt, H. L. (1990). The Tin Peddler Story. Sharon Cowen. Berne, Indiana.

Schuller, R. A. (2011). *When You Are Down to Nothing, God Is Up to Something. Van Wert Bulletin.*New York: Faith Words.

Stephenson, J. (2013-2018). Photo and letter, emails, and conversations.

Sutton. (1882). MERCER COUNTY OHIO - BIO: Thornton Spriggs.(From "History of Van Wert and Mercer Counties,Ohio) Retrieved July 27, 2014, from The OhioBiographies Project: http:/files.usgwarchives.net/oh/mercer/bios/spriggs.txt

Van Tilburg, N. (2014, 2015;). Shanes Crossing Historical Society (S. Cowen, Interviewer) Rockford, Ohio.

Voskamp, A. (2010). *One Thousand Gifts*. Grand Rapids: Zondervan.

Wikipedia.org. (2015, June 21). Lollbach. Retrieved March 5, 2016 from Wikipedia, the free encyclopedia: http//en.wikipedia.org/wiki/Lollbach

Wood, D. [?]."Profile of the Sociopath."Retrieved August 1, 2013,from http://www.mcafee.cc/Bin/sb.html: